Johannesburg
& Mpumalanga
3 to 10-day plan| Google Maps|
Local Tips

Contents

1 Introduction

Brimming with vibrant culture, inspiring history, and contemporary flair, Johannesburg – South Africa's largest city – opens its arms to visitors from around the globe, enticing them with a unique blend of rich traditions and cosmopolitan charm. Known as the "City of Gold" for its roots in the gold mining industry, Johannesburg stands today as an economic powerhouse and an influential player in the international arena, making it a must-visit destination for every intrepid traveler.

Stepping into Johannesburg, you're greeted with a pulsating energy that's both captivating and infectious. The city, fondly referred to as "Jozi" by locals, is a melting pot of cultures, a testament to its diverse population. Here, the blend of languages, cuisines, and traditions forms a colorful tapestry that tells a story of a society rich in diversity and brimming with resilience. Delve into Johannesburg's compelling past by visiting the Apartheid Museum, where the narratives of South Africa's tumultuous past are told with authenticity and raw emotion. The Constitution Hill, once a site of incarceration and now a beacon of South Africa's democratic freedoms, is another must-see. Johannesburg is not just about remembering the past, but also about celebrating the lessons learned and the progress made.

The city also thrives on creativity and the arts. Neighborhoods like Maboneng and Braamfontein are burgeoning cultural hubs, adorned with vivid street art, chic cafes, and avant-garde galleries. Visit the Museum of African Design for a taste of the continent's innovative art scene, or lose yourself in the bustling markets, where handcrafted goods offer a tangible connection to this vibrant community.

Nature lovers are not left out in Johannesburg either. The city's green lung, the Johannesburg Botanical Gardens, provides a serene escape, while the nearby Cradle of Humankind offers a fascinating look into our ancient past. Additionally, the city serves as a gateway to some of Africa's finest wildlife reserves, including the world-renowned Kruger National Park.

Whether you're a history buff, a foodie, an art enthusiast, or an outdoor adventurer, Johannesburg offers an unforgettable journey of discovery. Its cosmopolitan spirit, coupled with its deep roots and resilience, offers an unforgettable travel experience that goes far beyond its glittering skyline. In Johannesburg, every street has a story to tell, and every corner invites exploration. Here, the past and the present intertwine in a dance that's as diverse as it is captivating. Visit Johannesburg and immerse yourself in the heartbeat of South Africa.

Enjoy embarking on this journey of the wonderful city of Cape Town in this Guidora Travel Guide.

1.1 History of Johannesburg

Johannesburg, fondly known as Jozi or the "City of Gold", is the largest city in South Africa. From its humble beginnings as a mining town to its present status as an economic powerhouse and cultural hub, Johannesburg has a rich and intricate history that mirrors the greater story of South Africa itself.

Early History

Before the arrival of European settlers, the region surrounding modern-day Johannesburg was inhabited by Bantu-speaking peoples. The fertile land and moderate climate made it ideal for farming and cattle herding. The name "Johannesburg" itself did not come into being until the gold rush era, named after Johannes Rissik and Christiaan Johannes Joubert who played a role in establishing the city.

The Gold Rush Era

Johannesburg's history is inextricably linked with gold. It began in earnest in 1886 when an Australian prospector named George Harrison discovered a massive gold reef on the Witwatersrand, a ridge that runs east-west across the Gauteng province. This discovery led to the establishment of the city of Johannesburg the same year.

Thousands of prospectors and fortune seekers from around the world, including Europe, America, and Australia, flocked to Johannesburg, setting off the Witwatersrand Gold Rush. The population of the town exploded, and within three years, Johannesburg had become the largest settlement in South Africa.

However, this boom came with a cost, and the native Africa populations were displaced and exploited.

The Apartheid Era

Johannesburg's history took a darker turn in 1948 with th establishment of apartheid, a system of institutionalized racia segregation enforced by the National Party governmen Johannesburg was deeply affected by apartheid laws, which led t forced removals of non-white populations from their homes t segregated townships on the outskirts of the city. The most notabl of these was Soweto (Southwestern Townships), which would late become a hotbed for anti-apartheid activism.

It was in Johannesburg that Nelson Mandela and other prominen anti-apartheid activists formed the military wing of the Africa National Congress, launching a campaign of sabotage against th apartheid government. Mandela was arrested and sentenced to lif imprisonment in 1964, largely for his activities in Johannesburg.

The Soweto Uprising of 1976, in which thousands of blac schoolchildren took to the streets to protest against the impositio of Afrikaans as a medium of instruction in schools, was a pivota moment in Johannesburg's history. The brutal response of th apartheid regime was broadcasted globally, putting Johannesburg a the forefront of the struggle against apartheid.

Post-Apartheid Era

The end of apartheid in 1994 brought a new chapter i Johannesburg's history. The city, like the rest of the country, wa faced with the challenge of reconciling its divided past and building shared future. This period saw the regeneration of the inner city which had suffered from neglect and high crime rates during th final years of apartheid.

Today, Johannesburg is a vibrant, multicultural city. It is th economic heart of South Africa and a significant player on th African continent. The city's history is evident in its landscape, fron the affluent, formerly whites-only suburbs to the bustling, informa economy of the townships.

Johannesburg is also home to several significant historical site related to the apartheid era, such as the Apartheid Museum and th former home of Nelson Mandela in Soweto. These places serve as poignant reminders of the city's tumultuous past and symbols of its ongoing journey towards social and economic equality.

Conclusion

The history of Johannesburg is a story of resilience and transformation, deeply intertwined with the broader narrative of South Africa. From its gold rush roots to its struggle against apartheid and beyond, the city has continually adapted and reinvented itself

1.2 The Population of Johannesburg

Johannesburg, the largest city in South Africa, is often referred to as the "melting pot" of cultures. This vibrant metropolis mirrors the ethnic, linguistic, and cultural diversity that characterizes the entire nation, reflecting a broad array of backgrounds and histories.

The population of Johannesburg is comprised of a myriad of ethnic groups. Predominantly, these are Bantu-speaking groups, including the Zulu, Xhosa, Sotho-Tswana, and Tsonga people, each bringing distinct languages and traditions to the city's cultural mosaic. Johannesburg also has a significant Afrikaner population, descendants of Dutch, German, and French settlers, whose influence is seen in the city's architecture and cultural practices. The English-speaking white community, largely descended from British colonists, also makes up a part of the city's demographic.

One unique and important aspect of Johannesburg's population is its substantial immigrant community. The city attracts people from all over the African continent, drawn by its economic opportunities and status as a global city. Immigrants from countries like Zimbabwe, Mozambique, Malawi, and Nigeria add another layer to the city's rich cultural tapestry. There is also a significant population of people of Indian and Chinese descent, largely descended from workers brought to South Africa during the colonial era.

The diversity of Johannesburg is not only ethnic and cultural but also socio-economic. The city encompasses affluent suburbs like Sandton, middle-income areas, and economically disadvantaged townships such as Soweto and Alexandra. These varying living conditions reflect the economic disparity that remains a critical issue in Johannesburg and South Africa more broadly.

This broad array of cultures, languages, and backgrounds significantly influences Johannesburg's character. The city is a blend of traditional African, Western, Eastern, and other global influences, resulting in a unique fusion that is evident in everything from its food and music to fashion and art. One can hear a plethora of languages spoken in Johannesburg, from Zulu and Sotho to English and Afrikaans, as well as languages from other African countries.

The diversity in Johannesburg, however, goes beyond simple coexistence. It is a dynamic, interactive phenomenon that shapes and is shaped by the city's social, economic, and political life. Despite the challenges that come with such diversity, including socio-economic inequality and occasional intergroup tensions, Johannesburg remains a compelling illustration of the multicultural face of urban Africa.

1.3 Languages and common phrases

As a multicultural city, there are a variety of languages spoken by the locals in Johannesburg. The most widely spoken languages in the city are Zulu, English, Sotho, and Afrikaans, reflecting the diverse ethnic makeup of its population. However, in total, Johannesburg residents speak all 11 of South Africa's official languages, and numerous others brought by immigrants from across Africa and beyond.

Zulu is the most commonly spoken home language in Johannesburg. It is one of South Africa's 11 official languages and belongs to the Nguni subgroup of Bantu languages. A common phrase in Zulu is "Sawubona", which means "Hello".

English is also widely spoken in Johannesburg. It is the primary language used in corporate settings, the media, and education. English in South Africa is characterized by a unique accent and the incorporation of words and phrases from other South African languages.

Sotho, or more specifically Southern Sotho (Sesotho), is another major language in Johannesburg. It is part of the Sotho-Tswana group of Bantu languages. "Dumela" is a common greeting, meaning "Hello" in Sotho.

Afrikaans, derived from Dutch and spoken by the Afrikaner population, is also commonly heard in Johannesburg. It has contributed many words to South African English. A well-known Afrikaans phrase is "Hoe gaan dit?" meaning "How's it going?".

The diverse population of Johannesburg also speaks languages like Xhosa, Tswana, and Tsonga, each with its unique phrases and expressions. Furthermore, with a significant number of immigrants from other parts of Africa, languages such as French, Portuguese, Swahili, and others native to Ethiopia, Somalia, and Zimbabwe are also spoken in the city.

In addition to the multiple languages, Johannesburg locals have developed a colloquial language known as Tsotsitaal. Originally a criminal argot, Tsotsitaal has become popular among the younger generation and is a mixture of several languages, including Zulu, Sotho, and Afrikaans.

A unique phrase often heard in Johannesburg is "Eish!", an interjection used across South Africa, expressing surprise, frustration, or resignation. Another is "Howzit?", a contraction of "How is it going?" which is a common informal greeting.

Overall, the variety of languages spoken in Johannesburg represents the city's rich cultural diversity and makes for a fascinating linguistic landscape.

1.4 Geography and Climate of Johannesburg

Johannesburg, located in the eastern plateau area of South Africa known as the Highveld, stands at an elevation of approximately 1,753 meters (5,751 feet) above sea level. It's the largest city in South Africa, though it is not one of the country's three official capital cities. The city lies within the province of Gauteng, the smallest and most densely populated province in South Africa.

The city's geography is characterized by man-made forests, rolling hills, and the gold-bearing reef of the Witwatersrand upon which it's built. Despite the urban development, the area is known for its greenery, with Johannesburg often cited as one of the largest man-made urban forests in the world, boasting over 10 million trees.

The Braamfontein Spruit, a small river that runs through several of Johannesburg's suburbs, is one of the city's significant geographical features. Johannesburg does not have any substantial bodies of water, which is rather unusual for a city of its size. This is primarily because Johannesburg evolved from the gold mining industry, rather than as a settlement by a river or coastline.

Climate

Johannesburg enjoys a subtropical highland climate, influenced by its altitude. The city experiences two main seasons: a mild, dry winter and a warm, wet summer.

The summer season, from October to April, is characterized by hot temperatures that can reach up to 26 degrees Celsius (79 degrees Fahrenheit). Afternoon thunderstorms are a common occurrence during the summer, often providing dramatic displays of lightning and relief from the daytime heat. Despite the rainfall, summer days in Johannesburg are largely bright and sunny.

The winter season, from May to September, brings dry, sunny days and cool evenings. Night-time temperatures can drop significantly, occasionally reaching freezing point, although snow is extremely rare. Daytime temperatures during winter are mild, generally hovering around 16-19 degrees Celsius (61-66 degrees Fahrenheit).

Despite the city's relatively high altitude, the climate is temperate and mild for most of the year. The weather combined with the city's green spaces makes outdoor activities such as golf, soccer, rugby, cycling, and picnicking popular pastimes for Johannesburg's residents.

1.5 Best time to visit

The best time to visit Johannesburg largely depends on the activities you're interested in. Each season in Johannesburg has its unique charm and comes with its array of activities.

Spring (September - November)

Spring is a wonderful time to visit Johannesburg, especially if you're a nature lover. The city bursts into color with blooming Jacaranda trees painting the streets purple. The weather is warming up, but it's not too hot, making it the perfect time for outdoor activities such as visiting the Johannesburg Botanical Gardens or the Walter Sisulu National Botanical Gardens.

Summer (December - February)

Summers in Johannesburg are characterized by hot, sunny days and often afternoon thundershowers. The city slows down over the festive season, but there are plenty of indoor and outdoor activities. If you're visiting in summer, a trip to the Gold Reef City Theme Park or the Johannesburg Zoo could be on your list. Remember to pack a raincoat or umbrella for sudden showers.

The AfroPunk Festival usually takes place in December. It's a celebration of music, style, and culture, featuring a line-up of local and international artists. It's a fun-filled event that showcases Johannesburg's diversity and vibrancy.

Autumn (March - May)

Autumn is an ideal time to visit Johannesburg. The weather is mild, with less rain than the summer months, and the city's trees take on beautiful hues of orange and red.

This is a good time to visit the Apartheid Museum or Constitution Hill to learn more about South Africa's history without the harsh summer heat. There is also the Human Rights Day public holiday in March, which often includes various commemorative events and activities around the city.

Winter (June - August)

Winter in Johannesburg is sunny and dry, making it a great time to be outdoors. Although nights can be quite chilly, daytime temperatures are usually mild. This is an ideal time to visit the Lion Park for a safari adventure or a trip to the Cradle of Humankind, a UNESCO World Heritage site, where you can explore the ancient history of humankind.

The winter season also hosts the Encounters South African International Documentary Festival, an excellent opportunity for film buffs to catch local and international documentaries.

Regardless of when you choose to visit, Johannesburg has a rich offering of cultural, historical, and recreational activities all year round, and its welcoming people and vibrant atmosphere make an visit worthwhile.

1.6 Currency on South Africa

The currency used in South Africa is the South African Rand, denote as ZAR or R.

As for the exchange rates, they fluctuate daily due to marke conditions. Some rough estimates are:

1 US Dollar (USD) was approximately between 18 and 19 Sout African Rand (ZAR).
1 British Pound (GBP) was approximately between 23 and 24 Sout African Rand (ZAR).
1 Euro (EUR) was approximately between 19 and 20 South Africa Rand (ZAR).

Please note that these rates are subject to change and may var depending on where you exchange your money. It's always a goo idea to check the current rates before you travel or make an currency exchanges. You can check the current exchange rates o financial news websites, through online currency converters, or b contacting your bank.

1.7 Key attractions in Johannesburg

Apartheid Museum

The Apartheid Museum provides a powerful insight into Sout Africa's apartheid era. The museum uses film, text, audio, and liv accounts to provide a chilling insight into the architecture an implementation of the apartheid system, as well as the inspirin stories of struggle that brought it down. Visitors are assigned a racia identity on arrival and experience the museum from thi perspective, giving a personal understanding of the weight an reality of apartheid.

Constitution Hill

Constitution Hill is a former prison complex that tells the story of South Africa's journey to democracy. The site has witnessed a century of South Africa's history and includes the infamous Old Fort Prison Complex, where both Nelson Mandela and Mahatma Gandhi were held. It's now home to the Constitutional Court, an embodiment of South Africa's progressive constitution.

Gold Reef City

Gold Reef City is a popular amusement park and a gateway into the region's gold rush history. The park features a mix of thrilling rides, historical exhibits, and live shows. The star attraction is a tour into the gold mines that run underneath the park, offering visitors a rare glimpse into the city's gold mining heritage.

The Johannesburg Art Gallery

The Johannesburg Art Gallery, located in Joubert Park, is the biggest gallery on the sub-continent, with a collection that spans 17th-century Dutch paintings to contemporary African art. The gallery regularly hosts major local and international exhibitions, showcasing a diverse range of artistic expressions.

Market Theatre

Market Theatre is renowned worldwide for bravely putting on brilliant anti-apartheid plays during the apartheid era, functioning as a beacon of hope and resistance. Today, it still retains its political edge, housing three theatres, a bar, a bookshop, and an art and photographic gallery.

Mandela House

The Mandela House, situated in Soweto, is the former residence of Nelson Mandela and his family. The modest house is now a museum dedicated to preserving the legacy of Mandela's fight against apartheid. Visitors can see historical photos, awards, honorary doctorate robes, and other items from Mandela's life.

Neighbourgoods Market

The Neighbourgoods Market in the hip suburb of Braamfontein is an urban food market that celebrates Johannesburg's food and design culture. Every Saturday, vendors offer a variety of locally produced food, drinks, and crafts, often accompanied by live music.

Soweto

Soweto, an abbreviation for Southwestern Townships, is a sprawling suburb with a rich political history. Highlights include the Hector Pieterson Museum, Vilakazi Street (the only street in the world that was home to two Nobel Peace Prize winners - Nelson Mandela and Desmond Tutu), and the Orlando Towers, a decommissioned coal-fired power station that is now an adventure center.

The Cradle of Humankind

Located about an hour drive from Johannesburg, the Cradle of Humankind is a UNESCO World Heritage Site and one of the world's most productive and important paleoanthropological areas. The site has yielded some of the oldest and most continuous fossil records of human evolution, making it a significant destination for anyone interested in the ancient history of humankind.

1.8 Safety precautions

Like any major city, Johannesburg has areas of both safety and concern, and it's important to be vigilant and aware of your surroundings. Here are some safety precautions to follow:

Be Informed and Alert: Do some research about the areas you plan to visit. Consult with your hotel or local contacts about the safety of areas. Stay alert, especially in crowded places where pickpockets may operate.

Secure Valuables: Avoid displaying expensive jewellery, cameras, smartphones, or other high-value items that might attract unwanted attention. Use hotel safes to secure your valuables when you're not carrying them.

Be Careful After Dark: It's advisable to avoid walking around less populated areas at night, especially if you're alone. If you must, stick to well-lit, busy streets, or better yet, use a reliable taxi or rideshare service.

Use Reliable Transport: When using public transport, opt for reputable taxi companies or trusted ride-hailing services like Uber or Bolt. When driving, keep doors locked, and windows closed, and never leave valuables in plain sight.

Be Aware of Scams: Be wary of strangers approaching you with "too good to be true" offers or overly friendly overtures that may be distractions for theft.

Trust Your Instincts: If something doesn't feel right, trust your instincts. If you feel uncomfortable in a situation or location, leave and move to a safer area.

Emergency Numbers: Have the contact numbers for local emergency services. The general emergency number in South Africa is 112.

By taking these precautions, you can ensure that your visit to Johannesburg remains safe and enjoyable. It's important to remember that while Johannesburg has areas of concern, it also has areas of vibrant culture, rich history, and welcoming locals.

2 Getting to Johannesburg

2.1 Visa requirements for South Africa

Visa requirements for entering South Africa depend on your nationality. Many countries, including but not limited to the United States, Canada, the UK, Australia, and most EU countries, do not need a visa for visits up to 90 days. However, the visa exemption status can change, and it's important to check the current regulations before you travel.

For those who do require a visa, you'll need to apply in advance at a South African embassy or consulate in your home country. Requirements typically include a passport that's valid for at least 30 days beyond your intended departure date from South Africa, proof of sufficient funds, a round trip or onward ticket, and proof of accommodation. Some countries may also be required to present a Yellow Fever certificate.

For the most accurate and up-to-date information, it's always advisable to check with the South African consulate or embassy in your country or visit the Department of Home Affairs' official website.

Lastly, remember that immigration rules are subject to change, and the latest information should always be sought from official government sources.

2.2 Airports in Johannesburg

Johannesburg's primary international airport, O.R. Tambo International Airport, is the busiest airport in Africa and is well-connected to many global destinations. Airlines like South African Airways, British Airways, Emirates, Delta, KLM, and many others operate regular direct flights to Johannesburg from various parts of the world.

Flights to Johannesburg from Europe typically take 10-12 hours, while flights from North America can take between 15-20 hours depending on your city of origin. From Asia and Australia, flights generally range from 10-14 hours. Many flights from North and South America, and Asia may have a stopover in a hub like Dubai, Addis Ababa, or Frankfurt.

Once at O.R. Tambo International Airport, there are numerous options for getting to the city center, including taxis, car rentals, and the Gautrain, a modern high-speed rail service.

Lanseria Airport, another airport located to the north-west of Johannesburg, primarily serves domestic and regional flights.

2.3 Transportation from the airports

Once you have arrived at Johannesburg's O.R. Tambo International Airport or Lanseria Airport, there are several options for reaching the city center.

Gautrain

From O.R. Tambo International Airport, one of the quickest and most efficient ways to reach the city center is by using the Gautrain, a modern high-speed rail service. The Gautrain links the airport to Sandton, one of the major business districts, in around 15 minutes. From Sandton, you can switch trains to reach Johannesburg's city center. Note that you need to buy a Gautrain Gold Card to use this service.

Taxi

Taxis are available at both airports, but they can be a bit pricey. You can find the taxi ranks outside the arrivals area. Make sure to use authorized taxis only and agree on a fare before starting your journey. You can ask the airport information desk about the approximate fare to your destination.

Rideshare

Rideshare services like Uber and Bolt operate in Johannesburg, providing a convenient way to get to the city center. You can book a ride using their respective apps. The pickup location at O.R. Tambo International Airport is at the short-term parking area.

Car Rental

Several car rental companies have desks at both airports. If you're comfortable driving in Johannesburg, renting a car can provide more flexibility for your travel. Keep in mind that driving is on the left-hand side of the road in South Africa.

Shuttle Services

Some hotels and accommodation providers offer airport shuttle services, which can be a convenient option. Check with your hotel if they offer this service.

When choosing your mode of transportation, consider factors such as cost, convenience, and safety. It's also a good idea to plan your journey beforehand to make your arrival as smooth as possible.

3 Transportation around Johannesburg

3.1 Public transportation

Gautrain

The Gautrain is a state-of-the-art rapid rail network in Gauteng. The rail network introduces an innovative mode of transport to combat the issues of congestion in Johannesburg and Pretoria. The Gautrain travels at a maximum speed of 160 to 18 kilometers per hour. It operates between 05:30 and 20:30 daily an the trains depart at intervals of approximately 10-30 minutes. Th cost per trip varies depending on the distance, starting from aroun R21 for a short trip.

Rea Vaya BRT (Bus Rapid Transit)

Rea Vaya BRT is a bus service that operates in Johannesburg. It is fast, safe, and affordable transport system that is designed to lin Johannesburg, Sandton, and Alexandra. The buses operate fro 05:00 to 21:00 on weekdays and from 06:00 to 18:00 on weekend The cost per trip is around R6.20 for a short trip and up to R13.8 for a longer trip.

Metrobus

Metrobus operates in the city of Johannesburg. It has over 330 buse covering over 80 scheduled routes. The buses operate from 05:00 t 20:00 on weekdays. The cost per trip varies depending on th distance, starting from around R10 for a short trip.

Minibus Taxis

Minibus Taxis are the most common form of transport i Johannesburg and are used by the majority of the local populatio They operate in almost all areas and run from early morning unt late evening. The cost per trip is very affordable, starting fror around R10 for a short trip. However, they do not have a se schedule and can be a bit chaotic for first-time users. From a safet point of view it is better to use the Gautrain or bus services.

Uber and Bolt
Uber and Bolt (formerly Taxify) are also popular modes of transport in Johannesburg. They operate 24/7 throughout the city and the cost per trip varies depending on the distance and time of day. These services are convenient as they can be booked and paid for via an app on your smartphone.

Please note that while public transportation in Johannesburg is generally safe, it's always important to be aware of your surroundings and keep your belongings secure.

3.2 Car rentals

Hiring a car at OR Tambo International Airport is a straightforward process and offers a convenient way to travel around Johannesburg and the surrounding areas. Here's a general guide on how to go about it:

Choose a Car Rental Company: There are several car rental companies operating at OR Tambo International Airport, including international brands like Avis, Budget, and Europcar, as well as local companies. You can choose the one that best suits your needs in terms of price, vehicle type, and additional services.

Booking: It's recommended to book your car rental in advance, especially during peak travel seasons. You can do this online through the car rental company's website. During the booking process, you'll be able to choose the type of car you want, and any extras like GPS, child seats, or additional drivers.

Arrival: When you arrive at OR Tambo International Airport, you'll find the car rental desks in the arrivals terminal. If you've already booked, you'll just need to present your reservation details, along with your driving license and credit card.

Inspection: Before you leave the airport, inspect the car thoroughly for any existing damage and make sure it's noted on the rental agreement to avoid any disputes when you return the car.

Driving: Remember that in South Africa, we drive on the left-hand side of the road. Also, be aware of the local traffic laws and speed limits.

Return: At the end of your rental period, you'll return the car to the designated area at the airport. The rental company will inspect the car and settle the final bill.

Remember, each car rental company may have slightly different policies and procedures, so it's always a good idea to check the specific terms and conditions when you make your booking.

Some suggestions for car rental companies include:

Avis Car Rental
Website: www.avis.com

Budget Car Rental
Website: www.budget.com

Europcar
Website: www.europcar.com

Please visit their websites for more information and to make a booking. If you'd like to see something different, tell me more about it, and I can show you more choices.

3.3 Tour companies

There are a number of tour companies in Johannesburg that offer day trips as well as trips for longer periods. If you are interested in using a tour company for an organised trip, please read the below carefully.

Research: Begin by conducting thorough research on the various tours available. Look for tours that cater to your interests, whether it's wildlife, history, adventure, or culture. Here are a few suggestions for tour companies.

Hylton Ross Tours
Hylton Ross website (https://hyltonross.co.za/johannesburg-tours/)

Timeline Travel
Timeline Travel website (https://timelinetravel.co.za/)

Mount Zion Tours and Travels

Mount Zion Tours and Travel website (https://www.mountziontour.co.za/)

MoAfrika Tours
MoAfrika Tours website(https://moafrikatours.com/)

Book in Advance
Some tours, especially popular ones, can fill up quickly. Booking in advance will help ensure that you get the tour and the date that you want. It also often allows you to get a refund if you need to cancel, provided you do so within the tour company's specified timeframe.

Understand What's Included
Be clear about what the tour price includes. Does it include transportation, meals, entrance fees to attractions, and tips for guides? Make sure you understand all the costs involved.

Check Safety Protocols
Particularly important for adventure or wildlife tours, ensure the company follows all safety regulations and has necessary emergency procedures in place.

Verify Cancellation Policy
Understand the tour company's cancellation policy before you book. This is particularly important if your travel plans are not set in stone.

Consider Small Group Tours
Smaller group tours can often offer a more personalized and enjoyable experience, allowing more interaction with the guide.

Travel Insurance
Consider getting travel insurance that covers tour cancellations, particularly for more expensive tours.

Local Tour Operators
Consider using local tour operators. They often have a more intimate knowledge of the area and contribute to the local economy.

Responsible Tourism

Look for tour operators that practice responsible tourism. This could include respect for local cultures, support for local businesses, and conservation efforts.

Remember that while booking a tour can take care of a lot of the logistics and provide a wealth of information, you should always stay alert and aware, particularly in unfamiliar environments.

3.4 Driving in South Africa

There are certain rules to adhere to whilst driving in South Africa. This comprehensive guide should help you.

Driving on the Left

In South Africa, you drive on the left-hand side of the road, and the cars are right-hand drive. This is the opposite of countries like the US or continental Europe. If you're not used to this, take a little time to familiarize yourself before setting off on a long journey.

Driver's License

Foreigners need a valid driver's license from their home country, or an international driver's license, to drive in South Africa. Make sure your license is in English so that local authorities can understand it. If it's not in English, you should get an International Driving Permit (IDP).

Speed Limits

Speed limits in South Africa are typically 60 km/h in urban areas, 100 km/h on secondary roads outside urban areas, and 120 km/h on highways and freeways. Speed limits are strictly enforced, with heavy fines for violations.

Drinking and Driving

Drinking and driving is strictly illegal, with a maximum allowable alcohol blood content of 0.05%. This is roughly equivalent to one glass of wine for the average woman and one to two for the average man. However, the safest policy is not to drink and drive at all.

Seatbelts

It's mandatory for the driver and all passengers to wear seatbelts while the vehicle is moving. Failure to do so can result in a fine.

Mobile Phones

It's illegal to use a handheld mobile phone while driving. If you need to make a call, use a hands-free device or pull over to the side of the road.

Important Road Signs

Here are a few South African road signs that are worth noting:

- ***Speed Limit Signs***: These are red circular signs with a white center displaying the maximum speed limit in kilometers per hour.

- ***Stop Sign:*** Unlike in some countries, a stop sign in South Africa means that you must come to a complete stop before proceeding, not just yield.

- ***Yield Sign:*** This sign is an inverted triangle with a red border. It means you must give way to other traffic.

- ***No Overtaking Sign:*** This is a rectangular sign showing two cars side by side. The car on the right is marked with a cross, indicating that you may not overtake.

- ***Animal Crossing Signs***: These warning signs show the silhouette of an animal, such as an elephant or antelope. They indicate areas where wild animals may cross the road.

Driving in South Africa can be a great experience, allowing you to explore the country's beautiful landscapes at your own pace. Just remember to drive safely and responsibly, and always be aware of local driving laws and regulations.

Highways in Johannesburg

Johannesburg has a comprehensive highway system that can get you to most parts of the city and its surrounding areas. The N1, N3, and N12 are the primary freeways servicing Johannesburg, connecting it to Pretoria, Bloemfontein, and the West Rand, respectively. However, be aware that traffic can be heavy, especially during peak hours. Signage is generally clear but having a navigation system will help you navigate the roads more efficiently.

Using a GPS

A GPS is an incredibly useful tool when driving in Johannesbur especially if you're unfamiliar with the city. It can help you naviga the city's many highways and local roads and avoid getting lost i potentially unsafe areas. Many car rental companies offer vehicle with built-in GPS units, or you can use a smartphone app such a Google Maps or Waze. Make sure to update your maps before you trip for the most accurate directions.

Safety Aspects
While Johannesburg is generally safe for tourists, it's important to b aware of your surroundings and take precautions when drivin Always keep your car doors locked and windows closed, especiall when stopped at traffic lights or in slow-moving traffic. Do not leav valuables in plain sight in the car, as this may attract thieves.

Keeping Doors Locked and Windows Closed
Keeping your car doors locked and windows closed is a basic safet measure to follow anywhere, but it's especially important i Johannesburg due to the risk of "smash and grab" thefts. These occu when thieves smash car windows to grab valuables inside. Alway keep valuables out of sight, preferably in the trunk, and never leav your vehicle unattended with the engine running.

Driving at Night
Driving in Johannesburg at night requires extra caution. It' generally best to stick to main roads and avoid unfamiliar areas afte dark. Be aware that some roads may not be well lit, and pedestrian or animals may not be easily visible. If you're going to be out lat consider using a taxi or ride-sharing service instead of drivin yourself.

In conclusion, while driving in Johannesburg can be a great way t explore the city and its surroundings, it's important to tak precautions to ensure your safety on the road. Stay alert, follow th rules of the road, and enjoy your trip!

3.5 Safety precautions

While Johannesburg is a vibrant city with much to offer tourists, lik any major city, it's important to take certain precautions, especiall when out at night. Here are some safety tips for tourists:

Stay in Well-Lit Areas: Stick to well-lit, busy streets as much as possible, especially at night. Avoid walking alone in isolated areas.

Use Reputable Transportation: Use reputable taxi companies or ride-sharing services like Uber or Bolt when getting around at night. Avoid unlicensed taxis.

Be Aware of Your Surroundings: Keep an eye on your surroundings and be aware of the people around you. Avoid displaying expensive jewelry, cameras, or other valuable items that might attract attention.

Secure Your Belongings: Keep your belongings secure at all times. Don't leave bags unattended and keep your wallet and phone in a front pocket or a secure bag.

Stay in Safe Neighborhoods: Some neighborhoods in Johannesburg have higher crime rates than others. Do your research and stick to areas that are known to be safe, especially at night.

Use Hotel Safes: Use the safe provided in your hotel room to store passports, extra cash, and other valuables when you're not carrying them with you.

Follow Local Advice: Locals often have the best knowledge about which areas are safe and which should be avoided. Don't hesitate to ask hotel staff or other local contacts for safety advice.

Emergency Numbers: Keep a list of emergency numbers, including the local police and your country's embassy or consulate, in case of an emergency.

Remember, most visitors to Johannesburg have a safe and enjoyable trip. Taking these precautions can help ensure that your visit is a positive one.

4 Where to stay in Johannesburg

Johannesburg is a diverse city with a variety of interesting suburbs, each having its unique features and attractions. Before deciding where to stay in Johannesburg it is wise to first understand the different areas and suburbs in Johannesburg. Here are some of the key suburbs in Johannesburg:

Sandton: Known as the city's financial district, Sandton offers luxury hotels, upscale shopping centers like Sandton City and Nelson Mandela Square, and a vibrant nightlife scene. It's a great base for exploring nearby attractions like the Apartheid Museum and Johannesburg Zoo.

Rosebank: This trendy suburb is home to the popular Rosebank Mall, the African Craft Market, and the Keyes Art Mile, featuring contemporary art galleries and boutique shops. Rosebank is also well-connected via the Gautrain, making it convenient for getting around the city.

Melville: A bohemian neighborhood with a lively atmosphere, Melville is known for its cafes, restaurants, and bars. It's a great place for experiencing Johannesburg's vibrant nightlife and exploring quirky shops and art galleries.

Maboneng: Located in Johannesburg's city center, Maboneng has undergone a revitalization and is now a trendy district with hipster cafes, street art, and a thriving arts scene. The area is home to the popular Market on Main, which offers local food, crafts, and live music on weekends.

Newtown: Another vibrant area in the city center, Newtown is a cultural hub with theaters, art galleries, and museums. The Newtown Cultural Precinct is home to attractions like the Market Theatre and the Museum Africa.

Braamfontein: Situated near the University of the Witwatersrand, Braamfontein is a youthful and creative neighborhood with a range of cultural activities, trendy cafes, and art spaces. It's also home to the Neighbourgoods Market, a popular Saturday market offering food, crafts, and live music.

Parkhurst: Known for its leafy streets and charming cafes, Parkhurst is a trendy suburb popular among locals. It offers a mix of boutiques, restaurants, and galleries, making it a great place for a relaxed and enjoyable stay.

Fourways: Located in the northern suburbs of Johannesburg, Fourways is known for its entertainment complexes, such as Montecasino, which offers a range of dining options, theaters, and a casino. The area also has various accommodation options and is well-positioned for day trips to the nearby Cradle of Humankind.

4.1 Accommodation in Sandton

4.1.1 3-Star Hotels in Sandton

Signature Lux Hotel by ONOMO, Sandton
Signature Lux Hotel by ONOMO is a modern, vibrant hotel located in the heart of Sandton, South Africa. The hotel offers a comfortable and stylish stay with a variety of amenities to ensure a memorable experience.

The room rate per night starts from $70, offering great value for the quality of service and accommodation provided. The hotel is conveniently located at 135 West St, Sandown, Sandton, making it a perfect choice for both leisure and business travelers.

SCAN ME

For more information, you can visit their official website: Signature Lux Hotel by ONOMO

Garden Court Sandton City

Garden Court Sandton City, part of the Southern Sun Hotel Group, is a modern hotel located on the corner of West and Maude Street, Sandton in the heart of Johannesburg's metropolitan area. It offers a comfortable and convenient stay for both business and leisure

travelers. The hotel is situated in close proximity to the Sandton Convention Centre and Sandton City Shopping Centre, making it an ideal location for those wanting to explore the city.

SCAN ME

The room rate per night starts from approximately $70, providing excellent value for the quality of service and amenities. For more information visit the website Garden Court Sandton City.

Hotel Sky Sandton

Hotel Sky Sandton is a modern, smoke-free hotel located in the Sandown area. It offers a full-service spa and an outdoor pool for relaxation, along with two restaurants for diverse dining options. The hotel is conveniently situated just 0.2 miles from the Sandton Convention Centre and 0.3 miles from the Sandton City Mall. The Johannesburg Sandton Station is also just an 8-minute walk away, making it a great choice for travelers interested in exploring the city.

Average nightly price: $42.51 (USD)| Guest rating: 8.2 / 10.0
Star rating: 3.5
For more information or to book a room, you can visit the hotel's website at Hotel Sky Sandton (https://www.hotelsky.co.za/)

4.1.2 4-Star Hotels in Sandton

Radisson Blu Gautrain Hotel

The Radisson Blu Gautrain Hotel is a luxurious accommodatio located in the heart of Sandton, Johannesburg. It's convenientl situated just steps away from the Gautrain Station, making it an ide choice for travelers. The exact location is Corner Rivonia Road an West Street., Benmore, Sandton, Gauteng.

The hotel offers a range of amenities including a fitness cente outdoor pool, and a restaurant serving a variety of internation cuisines. Each room is elegantly furnished and equipped wit modern amenities to ensure a comfortable stay.

The room rate starts from $105 per night, providing excellent valu for its location and services. Whether you're in town for business c leisure, Radisson Blu Gautrain Hotel offers a comfortable and

convenient stay in Sandton. For more information please visit th website Radisson Blu Gautrain (https://bit.ly/3CLPzJ3).

Protea Hotel by Marriott Balalaika Hotel, Sandton

The Protea Hotel by Marriott Balalaika in Sandton is a luxurious an comfortable accommodation option for travelers. The hotel i located in the heart of Sandton's business, entertainment, and shopping district, making it a convenient choice for both business and leisure travelers.

The hotel offers a variety of amenities to ensure a comfortable stay, including a fitness center, a spa, and two outdoor pools. The rooms are
elegantly decorated and equipped with all the necessary amenities for a comfortable stay.

The room rate per night at the Protea Hotel by Marriott Balalaika starts from $105. For more details and to make a booking, you can visit their website Protea Hotel by Marriott Balalaika Sandton (https://bit.ly/43W9n8H)

Please note that the actual room and hotel facilities may vary. It's always best to check the hotel's official website for the most accurate and up-to-date information.

Southern Sun Katherine Street

The Southern Sun Katherine Street is a luxurious hotel located in the heart of Sandton, Johannesburg's premier financial and business district. The hotel is known for its excellent service, comfortable rooms, and a range of amenities designed to make your stay as enjoyable as possible.

The room rate per night is approximately $102, offering great value for the level of comfort and service provided.

The hotel is conveniently located at 115 Katherine St, Sandown, Sandton, 2146, South Africa. This location provides easy access to a

variety of local attractions, including Sandton City Mall, Nelson Mandela Square, and the Sandton Convention Centre.

For more information about the hotel, you can visit their website Southern Sun Katherine Street (https://bit.ly/3Pjg1kY)

Whether you're traveling for business or pleasure, the Southern Sun Katherine Street offers a comfortable and convenient stay in Sandton.

4.1.3 5-Star Hotels in Sandton

Saxon Hotel, Villas & Spa

The Saxon Hotel, Villas and Spa is a luxurious retreat nestled in the heart of Sandton, Johannesburg. This five-star hotel offers an unparalleled experience of elegance and sophistication.

The hotel is located at 36 Saxon Road, Johannesburg, 2196, South Africa, in the tranquil, tree-lined suburb of Sandhurst. It's just a short drive from the bustling business centers and shopping destinations of Sandton and Johannesburg.

The room rate per night starts from approximately $600, offering a blend of rich cultural history and contemporary five-star service.

For more details, you can visit their official website: Saxon Hotel, Villas and Spa (https://www.saxon.co.za/)

Experience the ultimate in luxury and relaxation at the Saxon Hotel, Villas and Spa.

Radisson Blu Hotel Sandton
The Radisson Blu Hotel is a luxurious 4-star hotel located in the heart of Sandton, a vibrant and upscale area in Johannesburg, South Africa. The hotel is within a 5-minute walk of Sandton City Mall and Peacemaker Museum. Nelson Mandela Square and Sandton Convention Centre are also within 10 minutes. The Johannesburg Sandton Station is only a 2-minute walk away, making it a convenient location for travelers.

The hotel offers a range of amenities including an outdoor pool, a restaurant, a fitness center, and free WiFi in public areas. A free area shuttle and a free shopping center shuttle are also provided for the convenience of guests.

The average nightly price for a stay at the Radisson Blu Hotel is $75.44 USD. Please note that prices may vary depending on the season and availability.

For more details and to book a room, you can visit their website Radisson Blu Hotel Sandton (https://www.radissonhotels.com/en-us/hotels/radisson-blu-johannesburg-sandton-gautrain)

Sandton Sun and Towers

Sandton Sun and Towers is a luxurious 5-star hotel located in the business district of Sandton, South Africa. It is conveniently situated just steps away from the Sandton City Mall and the Sandton Convention Centre. The Peacemaker Museum and Nelson Mandela Square are also within a 10-minute walk. The Johannesburg Sandton Station is a mere 7-minute walk away, making it an ideal location for both business and leisure travelers.

Here are some of the key features of the hotel:
It houses 2 restaurants and 2 outdoor pools.
A full-service spa is available for guests to unwind and relax.
The hotel offers free WiFi in public areas.
Other amenities include a fitness center, a bar/lounge, and valet parking.

The average nightly price for a stay at the Sandton Sun and Towers i approximately $149.00 USD. Please note that prices may var depending on the time of booking and room availability.

For more information or to book a room please visit Sandton Su Hotel (https://www.southernsun.com/sandton-sun-hotel)

Here is an image that might give you a feel of the ambiance at th Sandton Sun and Towers:

Michelangelo Hotel

The Michelangelo Hotel is a 5-star hotel that offers an experience c luxury and comfort in the heart of Sandton, South Africa. This hotel i not just a place to stay, but a destination that offers a rich an memorable experience to its guests. The Michelangelo Hotel is pa of the Leading Hotels of the World.

- The hotel is located in a shopping district, just steps away fror the Sandton Convention Centre and Nelson Mandela Square. Th Sandton City Mall is also just 0.2 mi (0.3 km) away, making it perfect location for those who love shopping and exploring th city.
- The hotel offers a full-service spa, an indoor pool, and an outdoo pool, providing a variety of relaxation and leisure options fo guests.

- The Michelangelo Towers also features a restaurant, a health club, and a bar/lounge, ensuring that guests have a variety of dining and entertainment options without needing to leave the hotel.
- The hotel is family-friendly and is conveniently located with the Johannesburg Sandton Station just 8 minutes by foot.
- The hotel offers free Wi-Fi in public areas and free self-parking, adding to the convenience of guests.

The average nightly price for a stay at The Michelangelo Hotel is approximately $270.98 USD. Please note that prices may vary depending on the season and availability.

For more details and to book a room, please visit the website Michelangelo Hotel (http://www.michelangelo.co.za/)

Davinci Hotel and Suites

he Davinci Hotel And Suites On Nelson Mandela Square is a luxurious 5-star hotel located in the entertainment district of Sandton, just steps away from Sandton City Mall and Nelson Mandela Square. The hotel is also conveniently located within a 5-minute walk from Johannesburg Sandton Station.

The hotel offers a full-service spa, an outdoor pool, a fitness center, and a restaurant. Free WiFi in public areas, free valet parking, and a free area shuttle are also provided for the convenience of the guests. The hotel is family-friendly and has a bar/lounge and a poolside bar for guests to relax and unwind.

The average nightly price for a stay at this hotel is $183.52 (USD). The hotel has received a guest rating of 9.0 out of 10.0, based on 553 guest reviews, indicating a high level of satisfaction among past guests.

What sets the Davinci Hotel apart is its prime location in the heart of Sandton, offering easy access to major attractions and transportation hubs. The hotel's array of amenities and services, including a full-service spa and a free area shuttle, provide a comfortable and convenient stay for both leisure and business travelers.

For more information about the hotel or to book a room please visit their website Davinci Hotel and Suites (https://www.legacyhotels.co.za/hotels/davinci-hotel-and-suites)

Interactive Map of Hotels mentioned in the Sandton area (https://bit.ly/46gZuE1).
Or scan below to get it:

SCAN ME

4.2 Accommodation in Rosebank

Rosebank is a cosmopolitan commercial and residential suburb in Johannesburg, South Africa. It is known for its vibrant atmosphere, with high-end shopping malls, cafes, restaurants, markets, and art galleries. Rosebank is also home to several multinational companies, making it a bustling business hub.

Some of the top-rated hotels in Rosebank are detailed below.

54 on Bath

54 on Bath is an upscale, chic boutique hotel located in the stylish Rosebank neighborhood of Johannesburg, South Africa. This hotel is particularly well-situated, with easy access to major tourist

attractions such as the Rosebank Mall, Rosebank Market, and the African Craft Market. It's also convenient for business travelers due to its proximity to Johannesburg's central business district. The hotel is directly linked to Gautrain Rosebank Station, making it incredibly easy to travel throughout the city.

The hotel itself exudes elegance and sophistication, featuring 75 guest rooms and suites each designed with attention to detail and equipped with modern amenities. Guests can look forward to plush furnishings, exquisite linen, and an in-room entertainment system. In addition to this, the hotel boasts a rooftop terrace with a swimming pool and lounge where guests can enjoy panoramic views of the surrounding neighborhood.

Rates vary from US$180 per room per night.. Please note that the rates do differ according to seasons and availability.

When it comes to dining, 54 on Bath does not disappoint. The hotel is home to the renowned Level Four Restaurant which offers a sophisticated menu of gourmet dishes made with fresh, locally sourced ingredients.

For more information and to reserve a room please visit the website **Southern Sun 54 on Bath(https://www.southernsun.com/54-on-bath)**

Southern Sun Rosebank

The Southern Sun Rosebank is a 4-star hotel that offers a comfortable and luxurious stay for its guests. It is conveniently located near the airport and is just a 10-minute walk from the Rosebank Station, making it an excellent choice for travelers.

Here are some highlights of the hotel:

- Features 2 restaurants, an outdoor pool, and a 24-hour fitness center.
- Offers free full breakfast and free Wi-Fi in public areas
- Has a bar/lounge, a poolside bar, and a snack bar/deli onsite

The average nightly price for a stay at the Southern Sun Rosebank is $80.77 USD. Please note that prices may vary depending on the time of booking and room availability.

For more information and to book your stay, you can visit their booking page at [Southern Sun Rosebank]

(https://www.southernsun.com/southern-sun-rosebank)

Radisson Red Johannesburg Rosebank

Welcome to the vibrant and stylish Radisson Red Johannesburg Rosebank!

Located in the heart of Johannesburg's trendiest district, Roseban this hotel offers a unique blend of modern design and high comfor It's the perfect base for exploring the city's rich history, culture, an buzzing nightlife.

The Radisson Red offers a variety of rooms to suit every traveler needs. The average room rate per night is around ZAR 1,500, whic may vary depending on the room type and the season.

The hotel is conveniently located just a short walk from th Rosebank Gautrain station, making it easy to explore the city an beyond. It's also within walking distance of the Rosebank Mall an the African Craft Market, where you can shop for local arts an crafts.

So, if you're looking for a stylish, comfortable, and convenientl located hotel in Johannesburg, the Radisson Red Johannesbur Rosebank is the perfect choice for you!

For more information or to reserve a room please visit the website a Radisson Red Johannesburg Rosebank (https://www.radissonhotels.com/en-us/hotels/radisson-red-johannesburg-rosebank)

Courtyard Hotel Rosebank

The Courtyard Hotel Rosebank, part of the City Lodge Hotel group, is a 4-star hotel located in the vibrant Melrose district of Johannesburg. It's just a 5-minute walk from The Zone @ Rosebank Shopping Center and Rosebank Mall. The Wanderers Stadium and Johannesburg Botanical Garden are also within 6 miles of the hotel. The Rosebank Station is only a 3-minute walk away, making it a convenient location for exploring the city.

The hotel offers a range of amenities including an outdoor pool, a bar/lounge, and a meeting room. Free Wi-Fi in public areas and free self-parking are also provided. Additionally, the hotel offers dry cleaning, laundry facilities, and a 24-hour front desk.

The average nightly price for a stay at the Courtyard Hotel Rosebank is $55.28 USD. Please note that prices may vary depending on the season and room availability.

For more information and to book your stay, please visit the hotel's webpage at Courtyard Hotel Rosebank (https://clhg.com/hotels/660/courtyard-hotel-rosebank)

Interactive map of hotels mentioned in the Rosebank area (https://bit.ly/3PoyIDZ)

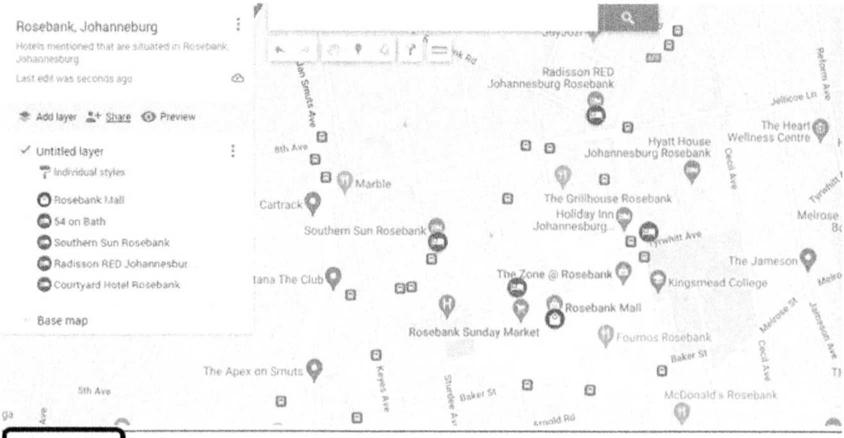

SCAN ME

4.3 Accommodation in Maboneng

This is one of the most successful urban-renewal projects in the world. Maboneng is a thriving cultural district with a mix of restaurants, coffee shops, art galleries, and retail stores. It's a great place to stay if you're interested in art and culture.

Although there is not many options for accommodation, below is a list of suitable choices for someone looking for a trendy, African experience.

CurioCity Accommodation Group

CurioCity is a hotel and hostel group that was launched in 2013 by a young man named Bheki Dube. At the time he was only 21 years old. His vision was to create safe and comfortable accommodation in Johannesburg. The type of accommodation varies from hostels to hotels, each being an African design which will connect with the traveller wanting to discover real South Africa.

The group has a number of types of hostels and hotels. The two places found in Maboneng are discussed below.

CurioCity Joburg Backpackers

CurioCity Joburg Backpackers is located in Fox Street in Maboneng in Johannesburg. The hostel offers a variety of room types from premium rooms, to standard double rooms and shared backpacker and hostel rooms. Prices range from US$12 per person for a shared room to US$48 for a premium room. The hostel features a balcony to watch the street life below, a hide-out bar, a chill lounge, free Wi-Fi and a jacuzzi. It is an ideal location to meet people, socialize and experience the vibe of Johannesburg.

For more information and book a room please visit their website at CurioCity Joburg Backpackers(https://curiocity.africa/johannesburg-backpackers-hostels/)

12 Decades Art Hotel

The 12 Decades Art Hotel consists of boutique apartments that chronicles the history of Johannesburg from 1886 to 2006. Each room is individually designed according to a specific theme from Johannesburg's history. Located in Fox Street in Maboneng in Johannesburg. Each apartment retails from US$50 per night.

For more information on the hotel to view the rooms, and to make a booking please visit the website at 12 Decades Art Hotel (https://curiocity.africa/12-decades-art-hotel/)

5 Dining in Johannesburg

5.1 Restaurants

Johannesburg is home to a myriad of wonderful restaurants. The city offers from the laid-back space to the brightly lit night lifestyle. Below is a list of a few choice restaurants. For more information about the various restaurants in Johannesburg visit the Eat Out magazine website Eat Out Magazine (https://www.eatout.co.za/restaurants/johannesburg-restaurants/)

Ethos

Located in Oxford Parks in Rosebank, this is a popular restaurant that offers simple family style Italian cooking. The restaurant has an outside seating area and a magnificent open plan bar area.
Location: Corner of Eastwood and Parks Boulevard, Oxford Parks, Rosebank
Contact number: 010 446 9906

Aurum Restaurant

An opulent environment with European cuisine, this is an excellent restaurant for dining with friends. Dishes are full of flavour, from starters to desserts.
Location: Leve; 7, The Leonardo, 75 Maude Street, Sandton
Contact number: 076 471 1489

Solo Restaurant

This is a contemporary dining area that celebrates all that is Africa, with an added enticing twist. The décor is opulent that reminds one that this restaurant s situated in the richest square mile in Africa. Well worth a visit.
Location: Shop 2A, Central Centre, Corner of Gwen Lane & Fredman Drive, Sandton.
Contact number: 010 100 8043

The Grillhouse Rosebank

The Grillhouse, one of South Africa's premium steakhouses, offers dining experiences filled with flavor. They offer perfectly aged steaks, succulent ribs, and outstanding wines.
Location: Shop 70, The Firs / Hyatt Shopping Centre, Oxford Road, Rosebank, Johannesburg.
Contact number: 011 880 3945

Marble Restaurant
Marble is a celebration of quintessential South African fare. It embodies South Africans' love of cooking with fire, a quality that makes their food culture different from the rest of the world.
Location: Trumpet on Keyes, Corner Keyes & Jellicoe Avenue, Rosebank, Johannesburg
Contact number: 010 594 5550

Momo Baohaus
Momo Baohaus serves Asian fusion dishes with a focus on Taiwanese steamed buns and bowls. The menu is filled with creative and flavorful options.
Location: 139 Greenway, Greenside, Johannesburg
Cuisine: Asian, Fusion, Vegetarian Friendly
Contact number: 010 900 4889

Pata Pata
Pata Pata is a local favorite in the Maboneng district. It offers a variety of African dishes with a modern twist.
These restaurants offer a range of culinary experiences from traditional South African barbecue to international fusion cuisine. Enjoy exploring Johannesburg's vibrant food scene!
Location: 286 Fox Street, Maboneng, Johannesburg
Cuisine: African, Contemporary
Contact number: 073 036 9031

5.2 Food experiences in Johannesburg

Besides eating out in Johannesburg one can embark on a guided eating tour. These tours not only offer a chance to taste a variety of dishes but also provide an opportunity to learn about the local culture and history. Enjoy your culinary journey in Johannesburg!

Soweto: Walking Tour with a Local Guide and Lunch
Type of Food: Local South African cuisine
Location: Soweto

Average Price per Head: $34.25 USD
Description: Learn the history of Soweto and experience the everyday life in the township. The tour includes a lunch where you can taste local dishes and experience the modern culture of Soweto.

For more information and to make a booking please visit Soweto Walking Tour.

Johannesburg: Taste of Africa Food Tour

Type of Food: Variety of local and international foods
Location: Yeoville or Maboneng| Average Price per Head: $39.39 USD

Description: Explore Johannesburg and discover the wide variety of African cuisines in the area. The tour takes you through either the suburb of Yeoville or Maboneng where you can taste a variety of local and international foods.
For more information and to make a booking please visit Taste of Africa Food Tour (https://bit.ly/3XquM7x)

Johannesburg: Lesedi Cultural Village Experience
Type of Food: Traditional African cuisine
Location: Lesedi Cultural Village
Average Price per Head: $134.16 USD
Description: Enjoy an authentic African experience on this half-day tour where you will visit a Lesedi Cultural Village, allowing you to enjoy this rich African culture first hand.

For more information and to make a booking please visit Lesedi Cultural Village Experience (https://bit.ly/3CGG4v2)

6 Top Attractions in Johannesburg and Surrounds

6.1 Gold Reef City

Gold Reef City is a premier entertainment destination in the south of Johannesburg, South Africa. It is reminiscent of an authentic turn-of-the-century mining town, which is conveniently located close to the centre of Johannesburg. Gold Reef City provides both locals and tourists with an escape into the city's mining past.

Attractions at Gold Reef City

Gold Reef City is home to a variety of attractions, each offering unique experiences that you will not find anywhere else. The theme park is packed with exhilarating thrill rides, numerous historical attractions, and a multitude of entertainment options. From the adrenaline-pumping Anaconda and Tower of Terror rides to the ever-popular Gold Panning experience, there is something for everyone. For those interested in history, the Gold Reef City Museum offers a glimpse into the gold rush days of Johannesburg.

Cost to Enter Gold Reef City

The cost to enter Gold Reef City varies depending on the type of ticket purchased. There are different prices for thrill rides, major rides, and non-rider tickets. It is best to check the official Gold Reef City website for the most up-to-date pricing information Gold Reef City (https://www.goldreefcity.co.za/)

Entertainment at Gold Reef City

Gold Reef City is not just about the rides and history. It is also a hub of entertainment. The complex houses a state-of-the-art casino for those feeling lucky, as well as a 4D theatre that offers a unique viewing experience. For the younger ones, there is a dedicated KidZone where they can enjoy a variety of fun and educational activities. The park also hosts regular live shows, including musicals and comedy acts, providing entertainment for all ages.

Dining at Gold Reef City

Gold Reef City offers a variety of dining options to suit all tastes and budgets. From fast food to fine dining, there's something for everyone. Here are a few options:

Barney's Restaurant and Bar

This family-friendly restaurant offers a variety of dishes, including burgers, pizzas, and steaks. It's a great place to relax and enjoy a meal after a day of exploring the park.

Boston BBQ

Boston BBQ is a bustling buffet restaurant, well known for its extensive selection of dishes. The buffet includes everything from succulent meats to mouth-watering desserts.

Mugg & Bean

For those looking for a lighter meal or a quick coffee break, Mugg & Bean offers a range of sandwiches, salads, and baked goods, as well as a wide selection of hot and cold beverages.

Ocean Basket
Seafood lovers will enjoy Ocean Basket, a popular South African restaurant chain that offers a variety of fish and shellfish dishes.

Fast Food
For those on the go, Gold Reef City has a number of fast food outlets including popular chains like McDonald's and KFC. There is also a food court offering a variety of quick and easy options.

Sweet Treats
For those with a sweet tooth, there are several options for dessert or a sweet treat. Candylicious offers a wide range of candies and chocolates, while Milky Lane serves up delicious ice creams and sundaes.

Remember, dining options can change and it's always a good idea to check the Gold Reef City website at Gold Reef City(https://www.goldreefcity.co.za/) for the most up-to-date information. Regardless of what you are in the mood for, you're sure to find something delicious to eat at Gold Reef City.

Gold Reef City is a vibrant and exciting destination that offers a unique blend of history, thrills, and entertainment. Whether you are an adrenaline junkie, a history buff, or just looking for a fun day out, Gold Reef City has something to offer everyone.

6.2 Cradle of Humankind

The Cradle of Humankind is a World Heritage Site located about 50 km northwest of Johannesburg, South Africa. This site is internationally recognized for its exceptional paleoanthropological record that casts light on the history and evolution of humankind over the last 3.5 million years.

The Cradle of Humankind is one of the richest sources of hominid fossils in the world, with the Sterkfontein Caves being the most famous within the site. The Sterkfontein Caves have yielded some of the most significant discoveries, including the first adult Australopithecus, the first near-complete skeleton of an early Australopithecine, and the remains of the 2.3 million-year-old Homo habilis, among others.

Visitors to the Cradle of Humankind can explore the Sterkfontein Caves and the Maropeng Visitor Centre. The Maropeng Visitor Centre is an exciting, world-class exhibition, focusing on the development of humans and our ancestors over the past few million years.

There are several tours available for tourists to explore this significant site. For instance, there is a day trip to the Cradle of Humankind that includes a game drive. This is a full day guided day trip from Johannesburg, including a 4x4 game drive in the Bothongo Rhino & Lion Nature Reserve, and a visit to the Sterkfontein Caves and Maropeng Museum.

The Cradle of Humankind is located near the town of Krugersdorp, with other nearby towns including Muldersdrift and Magaliesburg. These towns offer a variety of accommodation, restaurant, and shopping options for tourists.

Visiting the Cradle of Humankind provides a fascinating insight into the complex history of human evolution, making it a must-visit destination for anyone interested in our collective past.

Please note that it's always a good idea to check the official websites or contact the local tourism authorities for the most up-to-date information regarding entrance fees, opening hours, and any travel advisories.

6.3 Pilanesberg National Park

Pilanesberg National Park is one of the most accessible South Africa National Parks. It is located in the North West Province and is less tha two hours' drive from Johannesburg, and about two and a half hour from Pretoria. The reserve is situated in the crater of a long extinc volcano, one of the largest volcanic complexes of its kind in the world The unique rock types and structure make it a unique geologic feature.

The park ranks among the largest of the parks in South Africa an covers an area of 55,000 hectares. The beauty of Pilanesberg i reflected in a large central lake, the Mankwe Dam. Over time, win and water have carved a spectacular landscape with rocky outcrop open grasslands, wooded valleys and thickets.

Pilanesberg National Park accommodates virtually every mammal c southern Africa and is also home to the Big Five, namely lior elephant, buffalo, leopard, and rhino. A wide diversity of birdlife i also found here.

Tours in Pilanesberg National Park

There are numerous tour operators that offer guided tours t Pilanesberg National Park. These tours can range from day trips t overnight stays. Some of the tours offer specialized experiences such as hot air balloon flights over the park, walking safaris, and bird watching tours. Personal tours can be arranged with private guides who have extensive knowledge of the park and its wildlife.

Traveling to Pilanesberg National Park

The distance from Johannesburg to Pilanesberg National Park is approximately 200 kilometers or about 125 miles. The journey can be made by car or by organized tour.

If you're driving, the journey will take you about 2.5 to 3 hours, depending on traffic and the exact start and end points of your trip. The most straightforward route is to take the N1 highway from Johannesburg to the R512 exit. From there, you follow the R512 northwest to the park.

If you are not comfortable driving, there are many tour operators that offer transportation from Johannesburg to Pilanesberg National Park. These tours often include pickup and drop-off at your hotel in Johannesburg, and they can be a stress-free and convenient way to visit the park.

Please note that travel times can vary based on factors like traffic and weather conditions, so it's always a good idea to allow extra time for your journey.

Traveling from Sandton to Pilanesberg National Park and Sun City (https://bit.ly/43Pki48)

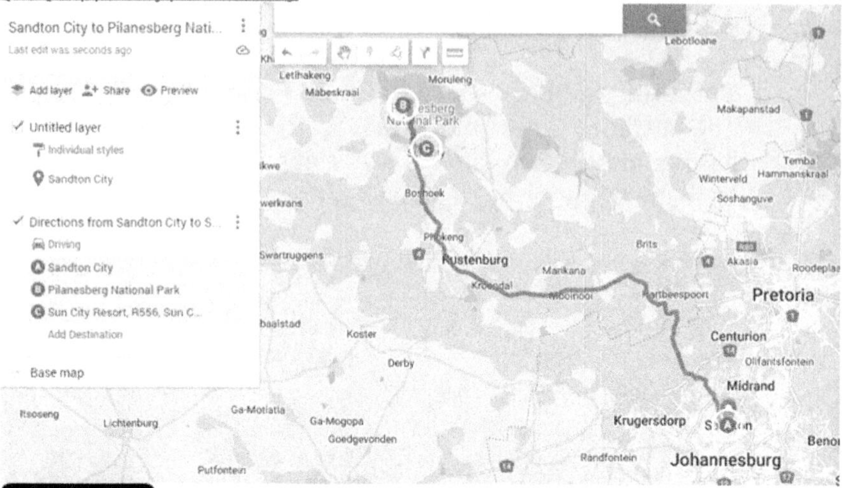

SCAN ME

Accommodation at Sun City

Sun City, part of the Sun International Hotel Group, is a luxury resort and casino situated in the North West Province of South Africa, near the city of Rustenburg, and is close to the Pilanesberg National Park. The resort offers a variety of accommodation options, ranging from budget-friendly to luxury.

The Palace of the Lost City

The Palace of the Lost City is a luxurious five-star hotel located in Sun City. It's designed to echo an ancient royal residence, nestled within the scenic beauty of the Pilanesberg mountains. The hotel offers a variety of room types, including luxury rooms, superior luxury rooms, and suites. Each room is exquisitely decorated, reflecting the unique setting of the hotel.

The Palace of the Lost City hosts several restaurants, including the Crystal Court for sumptuous breakfasts and high tea, and the Plume for a sophisticated dining experience. The average room rate at The Palace of the Lost City can vary greatly depending on the season and room type, but it is generally in the higher price range due to its luxury status.

Sun City Hotel

The Sun City Hotel is at the heart of the Sun City Resort and is a vibrant hub of activity. It offers a variety of room types, including luxury twin rooms, luxury family rooms, and suites. The rooms are modern and comfortable, providing a relaxing place to rest after a day of activities.

The Sun City Hotel is home to the Sun Terrace, which offers a variety of buffet options, and the Harlequin's cocktail bar. The average room rate at the Sun City Hotel is more moderate compared to The Palace of the Lost City, but it can vary depending on the season and room type.

Cascades

The Cascades is a tranquil retreat nestled in a secluded garden environment within the Sun City Resort. It offers a variety of room types, including luxury rooms, superior luxury rooms, and suites. The rooms are elegantly decorated and come with all the amenities for a comfortable stay.

The Cascades hosts the Peninsula, a fine dining restaurant offering a variety of dishes. The average room rate at The Cascades can vary, but it generally offers a balance between luxury and affordability.

Cabanas

The Cabanas is the most affordable hotel within the Sun City Resort. It offers standard and family rooms, all of which are modern, comfortable, and provide great value for money.

The Cabanas hosts the Palm Terrace, which offers a variety of buffet options. The average room rate at The Cabanas is the most affordable within the Sun City Resort, making it a great option for budget-conscious travelers.

Please note that room rates can vary greatly depending on the season, room type, and availability. Please visit the Sun City website

as Sun City(https://www.suninternational.com/sun-city/accommodation/) to find out more information and to check the latest rates and availability.

6.4 Kruger National Park in Mpumalanga

Kruger National Park is one of the largest game reserves in Africa, located in north-eastern South Africa. It spans across the provinces of Limpopo and Mpumalanga, stretching 360 kilometers from north to south and 65 kilometers from east to west. The park is part of the Kruger to Canyons Biosphere, an area designated by UNESCO as an International Man and Biosphere Reserve.

The park is home to a high density of wild animals, including the Bi 5: lions, leopards, rhinos, elephants, and buffalos. It is also home to

diverse bird population and numerous species of reptile

amphibians, and fish. The park's vegetation varies from dense woodland to open savannah, providing a habitat for a wide range of wildlife.

Different Parts of the Park and Vegetation

Kruger National Park is divided into six ecosystems: Baobab sandveld, Mopane scrub, Lebombo knobthorn-marula bushveld, mixed acacia thicket, Combretum-silver clusterleaf, and riverine forest. Each of these ecosystems supports a unique combination of plant and animal life.

Weather in the Kruger National Park

The weather in Kruger National Park varies throughout the year. The summer months (October to March) are hot and humid with frequent rain showers, while the winter months (April to September) are dry and mild. The best time to visit for wildlife viewing is during the dry winter months when animals congregate around water sources.

Kruger National Park is divided into several rest camps, each offering different types of accommodation and facilities. Some of the main camps include:

Skukuza: The largest camp, with a variety of accommodation options, including bungalows, cottages, and guest houses. Facilities include a shop, restaurant, fuel station, and swimming pool.

Satara: Known for its high concentration of lions, Satara offers bungalows and guest cottages. Facilities include a shop, restaurant, and fuel station.

Lower Sabie: This camp offers guest houses, bungalows, and safari tents. It is located on the banks of the Sabie River, providing excellent game viewing opportunities.

Olifants: Perched on a hill overlooking the Olifants River, this camp offers bungalows and guest houses. The view from this camp is a highlight.

Berg-en-Dal: Located in the hills of the "Mountain Bushveld", this camp offers bungalows and guest cottages. It is known for its beautiful surroundings and large herds of antelope.

Pretoriuskop: The oldest rest camp in the park, offering bungalows, family cottages, and guest houses. The camp is situated in wooded hills and is known for its rich plant life.
Each camp offers a unique experience and different opportunities for game viewing. Accommodation ranges from basic to luxury, catering to a variety of budgets and preferences.

Traveling to the Kruger National Park
Traveling from Sandton to Kruger National Park can be done by road or air. The drive is approximately 450 kilometers and takes about 5-6 hours. There are also regular flights from Johannesburg to Skukuza Airport, located inside the park, and from there you can rent a car or take a shuttle to your chosen camp.

For detailed information about each camp's accommodation and facilities, please visit the official Kruger National Park website at Kruger National Park bookings (https://www.sanparks.org/parks/kruger). It is important to book accommodation far in advance to secure a space.

7 Culture and Entertainment in Johannesburg

7.1 Art Galleries

Johannesburg Art Gallery

The Johannesburg Art Gallery is located at the corner of Klein and King George Streets, in Joubert Park, Johannesburg. This location is in the city centre of Johannesburg. The gallery is proud to exhibit one of the largest art collections in South Africa. has a number of contemporary art pieces and exhibitions spread over 15 exhibition halls.

Opening hours: Tuesdays to Sundays from 10:AM to 5.00 pm.
Ticket price: Entry is approximately US$3 per adult.

7.2 Museums

Apartheid Museum

The Apartheid Museum is a powerful and moving journey through the era of apartheid in South Africa. Located in Johannesburg, it is a must-visit for anyone interested in understanding the country's history and the struggle for freedom that shaped its present.

The museum uses film, text, audio, and live accounts to provide a chilling insight into the architecture and implementation of the apartheid system. It also serves as a beacon of hope, showing the world how South Africa is coming to terms with its oppressive past and working towards a future that all South Africans can call their own.

One of the most impactful exhibits is the entrance to the museum itself. Upon entering, visitors are randomly assigned a racial identity, which determines which entrance they use and what experiences they encounter inside, effectively illustrating the arbitrary and dehumanizing nature of racial segregation.

Other notable exhibits include the pillars of the constitution, the segregation exhibits, and the Mandela exhibition. The museum also hosts temporary exhibits related to the apartheid era.

Location: Northern Parkway and Gold Reef Road, Ormonde, Johannesburg
Opening Hours: 9:00 AM - 5:00 PM, Tuesday to Sunday (Closed on Mondays)
Ticket Price: Adults - R95, Students/Pensioners - R80, Children (under 18) - R45
Top Exhibits: The pillars of the constitution, the segregation exhibits, and the Mandela exhibition.

The Apartheid Museum is not just a museum; it is a journey through a significant part of South Africa's history and a testament to the resilience and spirit of its people. It is a place that encourages reflection and dialogue and is a must-visit for anyone seeking to understand the complexities of South Africa's past and its ongoing journey towards reconciliation and unity.

Museum of African Design (MOAD)
MOAD is the first museum in Africa dedicated to design. Located in the vibrant Maboneng Precinct, it serves as a cultural hub for the exploration of African design across disciplines. The museum hosts a variety of exhibitions and events, showcasing the diversity and dynamism of African design, and fostering a deeper understanding of Africa's cultural heritage.

Location: 281 Commissioner Street, Maboneng, Johannesburg
Opening Hours: 10:00 AM - 4:00 PM, Wednesday to Sunday (Closed on Mondays and Tuesdays)
Ticket Price: Free entry
Top Exhibits: The museum's exhibits change regularly, featuring contemporary design across various disciplines including fashion, furniture, and visual arts.

South African National Museum of Military History

The South African National Museum of Military History is a fascinating destination located in Johannesburg. It is the only museum of its kind in South Africa and serves as a memorial for all South Africans who have served in the armed forces.

The museum offers a comprehensive overview of South Africa's involvement in military conflicts over the years. It houses an impressive collection of military hardware, including tanks, aircraft, and artillery, as well as a vast array of medals, uniforms, and memorabilia.

The museum's exhibits cover both World Wars, the Anglo-Zulu Wa the Anglo-Boer War, and the struggle against apartheid. One of tl highlight exhibits is the 'Messerschmitt Me 262', the world's fir operational jet-powered fighter aircraft used by the Germa Luftwaffe during World War II. Another notable exhibit is tl 'Osprey MK IV Armor', a type of body armour used by the Britis forces in Afghanistan.

Location: 22 Erlswold Way, Saxonwold, Johannesburg
Opening Hours: 7:30 AM - 4:00 PM, daily
Ticket Price: Adults – R50, Pensioners - R25, Children (under 18) R30
It's always a good idea to check the museum's official website c contact them directly for the most accurate and up-to-dat information.
Contact number: 011 646 5513

Whether you are a history buff, a military enthusiast, or just curiou about South Africa's past, the South African National Museum c Military History is a must-visit destination in Johannesburg.

Constitution Hill Human Rights Precinct

The Constitution Hill Human Rights Precinct is a living museum an a beacon of South Africa's hard-won freedom. Located i Johannesburg, it tells the story of South Africa's journey t democracy. The site is a former prison and military fort that bear testament to South Africa's turbulent past and, today, is home to th country's Constitutional Court, which endorses the rights of a citizens.

One of the most significant exhibits is the Old Fort, which was bui to protect the city of Johannesburg and was later used as a prisor Another notable exhibit is the Women's Jail, which tells the stories c the female political prisoners who were once held there. Th Number Four museum provides insight into the harsh condition under which prisoners lived.

Location: 11 Kotze Street, Braamfontein, Johannesburg
Opening Hours: 9:00 AM - 5:00 PM, Monday to Friday; 9:00 AM 4:00 PM, Saturday and Sunday

Ticket Price: Adults - R85, Students/Pensioners - R60, Children (under 18) - R40.
Contact number: 011 381 3100
It is always a good idea to check the museum's official website or contact them directly for the most accurate and up-to-date information.

The Constitution Hill Human Rights Precinct is not just a museum; it's a journey through a significant part of South Africa's history and a testament to the resilience and spirit of its people. It's a place that encourages reflection and dialogue and is a must-visit for anyone seeking to understand the complexities of South Africa's past and its ongoing journey towards reconciliation and unity.

James Hall Museum of Transport

The James Hall Museum of Transport in Johannesburg is the largest and most comprehensive museum of land transport in South Africa. It was established by the Late Jimmie Hall together with the City of Johannesburg in February 1964.

The museum is home to a vast collection of vintage transport, including classic and vintage cars, bicycles, motorcycles, carriages, trams, and trolley buses. One of the highlight exhibits is the impressive collection of steam-driven vehicles and a fascinating array of historical buses and trams.

The museum aims to preserve and promote the history of over 400 years of transport in South Africa in particular and Africa in general. It provides an opportunity for the public to see the development of transport from the use of animals, such as ox-wagons, to early steam-driven vehicles, and then to the motor cars of today.

Location: Pioneers' Park, Rosettenville Road, La Rochelle, Johannesburg
Opening Hours: The museum was open from Tuesday to Sunday, 9:00 AM – 4.30 PM.
Ticket Price: Entry to the museum was free

Hector Pietersen Museum

The Hector Pieterson Museum is a large museum located in Orlando West, Soweto, South Africa, two blocks away from where Hector Pieterson was shot and killed. The museum is named in his honor. It became one of the first museums in Soweto when it opened on 16 June 2002. A companion museum nearby is Mandela House, the former home of Nelson Mandela and his family, which has been run as a museum since 1997.

The museum covers the events leading up to, and during, the anti-Apartheid Soweto Uprising. The museum is centered around the consequences of the events of 16 June 1976, where a protest by school children in Soweto against apartheid-inspired education resulted in a wave of protests across the country known as the Soweto uprising. The iconic image of a black schoolchild shot by the police, Hector Pieterson, brought home to many people within and outside of South Africa the brutalities of the Apartheid regime.

Location: 8287 Khumalo St, Orlando West, Johannesburg, 1804, South Africa
Opening Hours: The museum is open from Tuesday to Sunday from , 10:00 AM - 5:00 PM.
Ticket Price: Entrance to the museum is free.

7.3 Theatres

The Lyric Theatre at Gold Reef City Casino & Theme Park
Located within the Gold Reef City Casino in Ormonde, this luxurious 1,100-seater theatre presents guests with top-notch entertainment live from their stage, including world-class theatre, performances from local and international musicians, ballet, comedy shows, and much more.

The Soweto Theatre

Situated in the vibrant cultural precinct of Jabulani, the Soweto Theatre provides a platform for up-and-coming talent to showcase Located in Brakpan, this venue hosts amazing concerts featuring international and local stars, sporting events, and even conference dinners and commercial launches. It also offers the ideal location for exciting must-attend events like the Great Moscow Circus and the Aussie Circus..

The Theatre of Marcellus at Emperors Palace

This 17-tiered auditorium offers theatregoers a lavish theatrical entertainment experience1.
their arts to the public and grow confidence in their craft. It hosts a lot of shows and events, making it the perfect venue to hire.

The Teatro at Montecasino

This theatre has played host to many world-class shows and performances from some of the best in the theatrical industry, including the internationally acclaimed St Peterburg Ballet, Chicago, The Rocky Horror Show, Katherine Jenkins, and Chris De Burgh. It can accommodate 1,870 people at full capacity and is considered to be one of the ten largest Lyric theatres in the world.

The Pieter Toerien Theatre & Studio at Montecasino

This small and intimate theatre, accommodating up to 390 people, is an ideal destination for top-notch comedy and live music. Notable performers include Tim Plewman, Alan Committie, Pieter-Dirk Uys, Marc Lottering, Moira Lister, and Bill Flynn.

The Theatre on the Square at Nelson Mandela Square

Located between The Butcher Shop And Grill and the Sandton Library, this vibrant 200-seater adds another dimension to the entertainment industry. Its location is ideal for enjoying a choice from a range of fine restaurants with international cuisine on the square or at the Michelangelo Hotel.

The Big Top Arena at Carnival City

The Big Top Arena at Carnival City is a renowned venue in Johannesburg, South Africa, known for hosting a variety of events, including concerts, theatrical performances, and other live shows. Here are some key features and details about the Big Top Arena:

- **Capacity**: The Big Top Arena can accommodate up to 3,500 people, making it a great venue for large-scale events.
- **Events**: The venue hosts a wide range of events, from music concerts featuring both local and international artists, to comedy shows, children's performances, and more.
- **Facilities**: The arena is equipped with state-of-the-art sound and lighting systems to ensure a high-quality experience for both performers and audiences. It also has comfortable seating and good sightlines to the stage from all areas.
- **Location**: The Big Top Arena is located within Carnival City, a popular entertainment complex that also features a casino, restaurants, bars, and a hotel, providing a comprehensive entertainment experience for visitors.
- **Parking**: Ample parking is available at the venue, ensuring easy access for visitors.

7.4 Nightlife

Johannesburg, often referred to as Jo'burg or Jozi, is a vibrant city with a bustling nightlife. Here are some of the top nightlife spots in Johannesburg and its suburbs:

Melville

Melville is a bohemian suburb known for its lively nightlife. 7th Street is the main strip where you will find a variety of bars, restaurants, and clubs. There is no specific entry cost for the area, but individual venues may have cover charges.

Maboneng

Maboneng is a revitalized district in downtown Johannesburg that's become a trendy hotspot for nightlife. The area is filled with art galleries, boutiques, and restaurants. At night, it comes alive with bars and clubs. The Living Room is a popular rooftop bar with great views of the city. Again, there's no cost to enter the area, but individual venues may have cover charges.

Braamfontein

Braamfontein is a central suburb that is popular with students and young professionals. It's home to numerous bars, clubs, and live music venues. Great Dane is a popular bar known for its hot dogs and dance floor. Kitcheners is one of the oldest bars in the city and hosts a variety of DJs and live acts. Entry costs vary depending on the venue and event.

Sandton

Sandton is a wealthy suburb known for its high-end shopping an nightlife. The area around Nelson Mandela Square is filled wit upscale bars and clubs. One of the most popular venues is Taboo, luxury nightclub that often hosts local and international DJs. Entr costs can be on the higher side due to the upscale nature of the area.

Rosebank

Rosebank is a cosmopolitan suburb with a variety of bars and club The area around the Rosebank Mall and The Zone@Rosebank i particularly lively. Katzy's Live is a popular venue for live music, an The Capital is a rooftop bar and club with great views. Entry cost vary depending on the venue and event.

While Johannesburg is a vibrant city with much to offer tourists, lik any major city, it's important to take certain precautions, especiall when out at night. Stay in well-lit areas, and never travel alon especially at night. Always use reputable transport, especially whe travelling to the centre of Johannesburg.

7.5 Shopping

Sandton City

Located in the upscale suburb of Sandton, Sandton City is one of th most prestigious shopping centers in Johannesburg. It offers a international shopping experience with over 300 retailers, includin high-end fashion brands, electronics, jewelry, and homeware store It's also home to a variety of restaurants and entertainment option including a cinema.

Rosebank Mall

Rosebank Mall is a cosmopolitan shopping center located in th trendy suburb of Rosebank. It offers a mix of high street an designer stores, as well as a variety of dining options. The mall is als home to the Rosebank Art and Craft Market, where you can find wide range of African artifacts, beadwork, leather work, woode carvings, and souvenirs.

Melrose Arch

Situated in the suburb of Melrose, Melrose Arch offers a uniqu shopping experience with its open-air design and moder architecture. It hosts a variety of high-end boutiques, a selection of restaurants and cafes. It's a great place t designer fashion, accessories, and homeware.

Nelson Mandela Square
Adjacent to Sandton City, Nelson Mandela Square is an iconic shopping center known for its large statue of Nelson Mandela. The square is surrounded by a variety of shops, from designer boutiques to art galleries, as well as a selection of restaurants and cafes.

44 Stanley
Located in Milpark, 44 Stanley is a mixed-use development that offers a unique shopping experience. It's home to a variety of boutique shops selling everything from fashion and homeware to books and antiques. The complex also hosts a number of restaurants, cafes, and art galleries.

The Mall of Africa
Situated in Midrand, between Pretoria and Johannesburg, The Mall of Africa is one of the largest shopping malls in Africa. It offers a vast selection of retail stores, including international fashion brands, electronics, sporting goods, and more. The mall also features numerous restaurants, a cinema, and other entertainment options.

8 3- Day Itinerary in Johannesburg and Pretoria

To follow is a three-day itinerary to visit Johannesburg and Pretoria.

A summary of the itinerary is:
Day 1: Soweto, Hector Pietersen Museum, Apartheid Museum, and Constitution Hill with lunch in Soweto
Day 2: Pretoria, Union Buildings, Cullinan Diamon Mine. Lunch in Pretoria.
Day 3: A tour of the Maboneng district, visit to the Museum of African Design, lunch at Pata Pata or another local restaurant, and the afternoon doing a bicycle tour of the area.

Interactive Map of the Directions for Day 1: Exploring Culture (https://bit.ly/3NF7tDA)

SCAN ME

Day 1: Explore Johannesburg's History and Culture

Morning: Start with Soweto
Begin your day early by taking a taxi or Uber from your accommodation in Johannesburg to Soweto. Aim to leave by 8:00 AM to make the most of your day.

First Stop: Hector Pieterson Museum
Your first stop in Soweto should be the *Hector Pieterson Museum*. This museum is dedicated to the 1976 uprising in Soweto and the tragic death of Hector Pieterson, a 12-year-old boy who became a symbol of the struggle against apartheid. The museum opens at 10:00 AM.

Second Stop: Vilakazi Street
Next, head to *Vilakazi Street*, the only street in the world that has been home to two Nobel Peace Prize laureates - Nelson Mandela and

Desmond Tutu. Here you can visit the *Mandela House Museum*, which was once the residence of Nelson Mandela.

Information about Vilakazi Street

Vilakazi Street in Soweto, Johannesburg, is one of the most famous streets in South Africa. It is renowned for its significant historical value, being the only street in the world that was home to two Nobel Peace Prize laureates - Nelson Mandela and Archbishop Desmond Tutu.

The Nelson Mandela House is one of the main attractions on Vilakazi Street. This is the former home of the late Nelson Mandela and his family, where he lived from 1946 to the 1990s. It is now a museum preserving his legacy, offering visitors a chance to experience his life story.

Another notable residence is Desmond Tutu's House. Although it's not open to the public, it's still a significant landmark as it's the home of the beloved South African social rights activist and retired Anglican bishop.

Vilakazi Street is also known for its vibrant atmosphere and cultural experiences. It is lined with numerous restaurants and shops where visitors can enjoy local South African cuisine, buy traditional crafts, and experience the lively local music scene.

Visiting Vilakazi Street provides a unique opportunity to delve into South Africa's rich history and vibrant culture, making it a must-visit destination for anyone traveling to Johannesburg.

Lunch in Soweto

After exploring Vilakazi Street, grab lunch at a local restaurant. *Sakhumzi Restaurant* is a popular spot that serves traditional South African cuisine.

Afternoon: Apartheid Museum

After lunch, take a taxi or Uber to the *Apartheid Museum*, which is about a 30-minute drive from Soweto. This museum offers an in-depth look at the history of apartheid through a series of powerful exhibits. Plan to spend at least a couple of hours here to fully explore the museum.

Evening: Constitution Hill

From the Apartheid Museum, take a taxi or Uber to *Constitution Hill*, a former prison complex that now houses the Constitutional Court. Here you can learn about South Africa's journey to democracy. The site closes at 5:00 PM, so aim to get there by 3:00 PM to give yourself enough time to explore.

After your visit to Constitution Hill, you can take a taxi or Uber back to your accommodation in Johannesburg.

Please note that this is a suggested itinerary and the times, order of attractions, and transportation methods may need to be adjusted based on your personal preferences, the location of your accommodation, and the operating hours of each site. Always check the latest information directly with the attractions and consider your safety when choosing transportation methods.

Day 2: Pretoria, The Union Buildings and The Cullinan Diamon Mine

This is a suggestion for a full day tour to see Pretoria, visit the Union Buildings and the Cullinan Diamon Mind.

Interactive Map for Day 2 of your 3-Day Itinerary(https://bit.ly/43RTeB1)

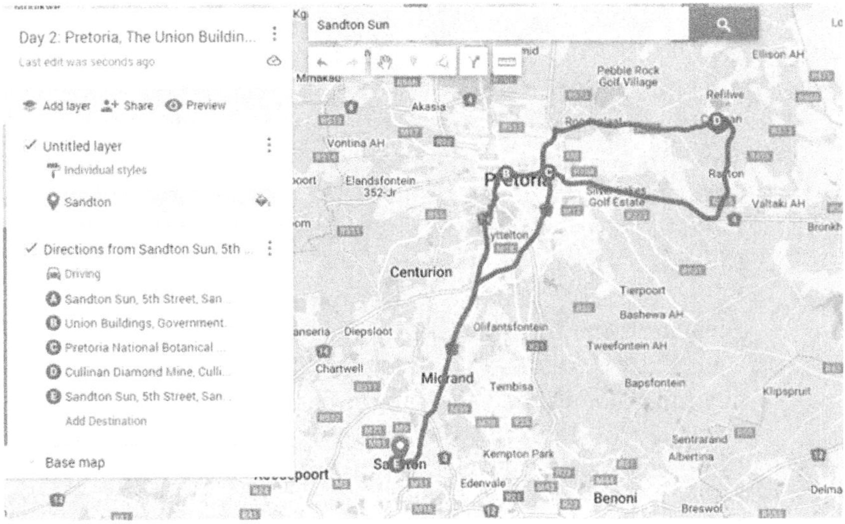

SCAN ME

Morning: Departure from Johannesburg
Start your day early by departing from Johannesburg to Pretoria. The drive should take approximately an hour. You can rent a car for the day or use a reliable taxi service.

Information about Pretoria
Pretoria, the capital city of South Africa, is known for its diverse culture and history. It is home to many historical sites, museums, and monuments that reflect South Africa's complex past. The city is also renowned for its beautiful Jacaranda trees, which bloom in a riot of purple every spring, earning it the nickname "Jacaranda City".

In addition to its political and historical significance, Pretoria is als an important academic city, hosting some of South Africa's to research institutions and universities, including the University (Pretoria and the Council for Scientific and Industrial Research.

Whether you are interested in history, politics, architecture, c nature, Pretoria and the Union Buildings offer a rich and divers experience for visitors.

Arrival at Pretoria

Upon arrival in Pretoria, your first stop could be the *Union Building* These impressive buildings serve as the seat of the South Africa government and also house the offices of the president. Th buildings are set in beautiful gardens, offering panoramic views (the city.

Information about the Union Buildings

The Union Buildings in Pretoria, South Africa, are a significar symbol of South African political history and a key tourist attractio Designed by the renowned architect Sir Herbert Baker, the Unio Buildings were completed in 1913, marking the union of th formerly separate colonies into the Union of South Africa. The Unio Buildings house the offices of the President and serve as the offici seat of the South African government. The buildings are a architectural marvel, featuring a mix of English monumental styl and indigenous South African influences. The buildings ar beautifully set within terraced gardens that offer panoramic views c the city.

One of the most notable features of the Union Buildings is the Nelson Mandela Statue. Unveiled on the Day of Reconciliation in December 2013, the 9-meter tall bronze statue commemorates the life and work of Nelson Mandela, South Africa's first Black president.

Pretoria, the city where the Union Buildings are located, is one of South Africa's three capital cities and holds significant importance. It is the administrative capital of the country, hosting many government departments and foreign embassies.

Next: Pretoria City Tour
After visiting the Union Buildings, you could explore other attractions in Pretoria. These might include the *Voortrekker Monument*, *Freedom Park*, or the *Pretoria National Botanical Garden*.

Lunch in Pretoria
For lunch, there are numerous restaurants and cafes in Pretoria offering a variety of cuisines.

Afternoon: Cullinan Diamond Mine
After lunch, make your way to the *Cullinan Diamond Mine*, which is approximately a 45-minute drive from Pretoria. Here, you can take a guided tour of the mine to learn about the diamond extraction process and the history of the mine.

Information about the Cullinan Diamond Mine

The Cullinan Diamond Mine is a renowned diamond mine in Gauteng, South Africa. It is named after the town of Cullinan where the mine is located. The mine has a rich history and is known for producing some of the largest diamonds in the world, including the famous Cullinan Diamond, which is the largest rough gem-quality diamond ever found.

The mine offers a surface walking tour where you can learn more about its rich history and see high-quality gemstones. The tour is called the "Pretoria: Cullinan Surface Diamond Mine Walking Tour". The tour is available from 10:00 AM. The entrance ticket costs start from US$ 8.58 per person.

Evening: Return to Johannesburg

In the late afternoon, begin your journey back to Johannesburg. You should arrive back in Johannesburg in the evening.

Please note that this is a suggested itinerary, and the exact route and schedule might vary depending on your personal preferences and the operating hours of each site. Always check the latest information directly with the attractions and consider your safety when choosing transportation methods.

Day 3: Self-guided tour of the Maboneng District

Interactive May of Day 3: Self-guided tour of the Maboneng District(https://bit.ly/3Xkx1cz)

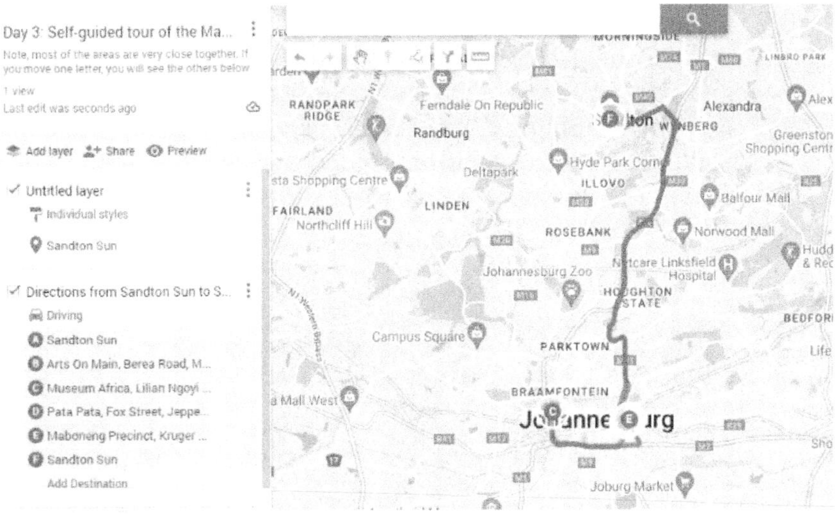

Scan me

Morning: Start at Arts on Main
Begin your tour at Arts on Main, a vibrant arts precinct in the Maboneng district. Here, you can explore various art galleries, artist studios, and craft shops. The area also hosts a popular market on Sundays.

Next: MOAD (Museum of African Design)
From Arts on Main, take a short walk to the Museum of African Design (MOAD). This is the first museum in Africa dedicated to design. MOAD hosts a variety of exhibitions and events throughout the year.

Lunch: Local Restaurants
For lunch, there are numerous restaurants and cafes in the Maboneng district offering a variety of cuisines. Pata Pata is a popular spot known for its African dishes.

Afternoon: Street Art and Architecture

After lunch, take a stroll around the district to admire the street art and unique architecture. Maboneng is known for its urban renewal and the area is filled with interesting murals and renovated industrial buildings. You can also spend the afternoon exploring the Maboneng Precinct with a Guided Bicycle Tour with Lunch for US$ 37.17. This revitalized district is known for its street art, boutiques,

and galleries. Do not miss the Arts on Main, a multi-purpose space that houses artist studios, galleries, and shops.

Late afternoon: Rooftop Bar
End your tour at one of Maboneng's rooftop bars, such as The Living m, where you can enjoy a drink with a view of the city.

Please note that this is a suggested itinerary, and the exact route and schedule might vary depending on your personal preferences and the operating hours of each site. Always check the latest information directly with the attractions and consider your safety when choosing transportation methods.

9 3 -Day Itinerary in Johannesburg and Pilanesberg

This is a different three-day itinerary which includes booked tours, and a self-guided tour. This tour includes Johannesburg and the Pilanesberg National Park.

A summary of the itinerary is:

Day 1: Soweto, Hector Pietersen Museum, Apartheid Museum, and Constitution Hill with lunch in Soweto
Day 2: Tour to Pilanesberg National Park
Day 3: A tour of the Maboneng district, visit to the Museum of African Design, lunch at Pata Pata or another local restaurant, and the afternoon doing a bicycle tour of the area.

Day 1: Explore Johannesburg's History and Culture

Book a full-day guided tour to visit Soweto, Apartheid Museum, and Constitution Hill.

Suggested Tour Companies

- Get your Guide(https://bit.ly/43NW0r2)
-
- MoAfrika Tours(https://moafrikatours.com/)
- Stephenson Adventures(https://stephensonadventures.co.za/)

Interactive Map for Day 2 of your 3-Day Itinerary(https://bit.ly/43RTeB1)

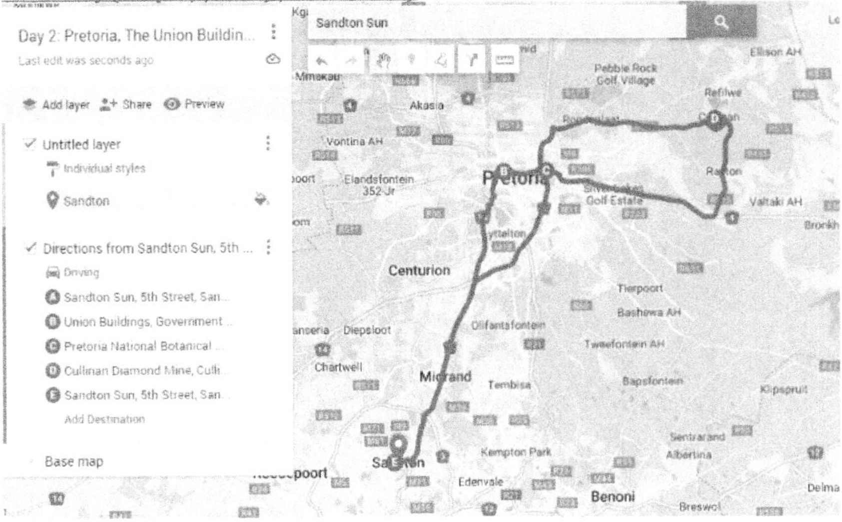

Morning

This tour typically starts in the morning around 8:00 AM. You will b picked up from your hotel in Johannesburg and driven to Sowet (South Western Townships), which is about a 30-minute drive.

First Stop: Soweto

In Soweto, you will visit the Hector Pieterson Museum, dedicated t a 12-year-old boy who was one of the first casualties of the Sowet uprising in 1976. You will learn about the events leading up to th tragic event and its aftermath.

Next, you will visit Vilakazi Street, the only street in the world th has been home to two Nobel Peace Prize laureates - Nelson Mande and Desmond Tutu. You can see the former home of Nelson Mandel which is now the Mandela House Museum.

Information about Vilakazi Street

Vilakazi Street in Soweto, Johannesburg, is one of the most famou streets in South Africa. It is renowned for its significant historic value, being the only street in the world that was home to two Nob Peace Prize laureates - Nelson Mandela and Archbishop Desmon Tutu.

The Nelson Mandela House is one of the main attractions on Vilakazi Street. This is the former home of the late Nelson Mandela and his family, where he lived from 1946 to the 1990s. It is now a museum preserving his legacy, offering visitors a chance to experience his life story.

Another notable residence is Desmond Tutu's House. Although it's not open to the public, it's still a significant landmark as it's the home of the beloved South African social rights activist and retired Anglican bishop.

Vilakazi Street is also known for its vibrant atmosphere and cultural experiences. It is lined with numerous restaurants and shops where visitors can enjoy local South African cuisine, buy traditional crafts, and experience the lively local music scene.

Visiting Vilakazi Street provides a unique opportunity to delve into South Africa's rich history and vibrant culture, making it a must-visit destination for anyone traveling to Johannesburg.

Lunch in Soweto

After exploring Soweto, you will have lunch at a local restaurant where you can try traditional South African cuisine.

Second Stop: Apartheid Museum

After lunch, you will be driven to the *Apartheid Museum*, which is about a 30-minute drive from Soweto. Here, you will learn about the history of apartheid through a series of powerful exhibits. The museum tells the story of apartheid from its inception, its development, and its demise with the election of Nelson Mandela as South Africa's first black president.

The tour typically ends around 5:00 PM, and you will be driven back to your hotel in Johannesburg.

Day 2: Tour to Pilanesberg Nature Reserve

This full-day safari tour takes you from Johannesburg to the Pilanesberg Nature Reserve. Here's a detailed itinerary and map.

Interactive map of Day 2: Day Trip to Pilanesberg(https://bit.ly/3qTJ1Wf)

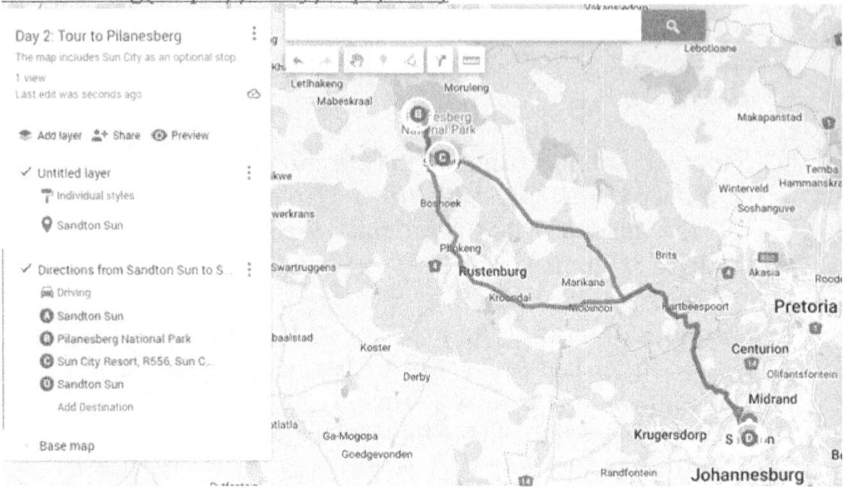

Scan me

Morning: Departure from Johannesburg

The tour departs from Johannesburg early in the morning. You will be picked up from your hotel by the tour company. The exact time of departure will be confirmed by the tour operator, but it's typically around 6:00 AM.

Arrival at Pilanesberg Nature Reserve

After a drive of approximately 2.5 hours, you will arrive at the Pilanesberg Nature Reserve. Here, you will join a ranger in an open vehicle for a game drive.

Game Drive in Pilanesberg Nature Reserve

During the game drive, you will have the opportunity to see a variety of wildlife, including lions, giraffes, cheetahs, hippos, and crocodiles.

The ranger will provide insightful commentary about the animals and their natural habitat.

Lunch in the Park

Lunch is typically included in these types of tours, but the specifics will depend on the tour operator. You might have lunch at one of the rest camps in the park.

Afternoon: Continue Game Drive

After lunch, you will continue your game drive in the park. This is a great time to spot more wildlife and take in the beautiful scenery of the park.

Evening: Return to Johannesburg

In the late afternoon, you will begin your journey back to Johannesburg. You should arrive back at your hotel in the evening.

The cost of the tour typically includes transportation, a guide, entrance fees to the park, and lunch. However, it's always a good idea to check the latest information directly with the tour provider. The starting price for this tour is approximately US$ 155.84 per person.

Please note that the exact route and schedule might vary depending on the tour provider.

Day 3: Self-guided tour of the Maboneng District

[Interactive May of Day 3: Self-guided tour of the Maboneng District(https://bit.ly/3Xkx1cz)](https://bit.ly/3Xkx1cz)

Morning: Start at Arts on Main

Begin your tour at Arts on Main, a vibrant arts precinct in the Maboneng district. Here, you can explore various art galleries, artist studios, and craft shops. The area also hosts a popular market on Sundays.

Next: MOAD (Museum of African Design)

From Arts on Main, take a short walk to the Museum of African Design (MOAD). This is the first museum in Africa dedicated to design. MOAD hosts a variety of exhibitions and events throughout the year.

Lunch: Local Restaurants

For lunch, there are numerous restaurants and cafes in the Maboneng district offering a variety of cuisines. Pata Pata is a popular spot known for its African dishes.

Afternoon: Street Art and Architecture

After lunch, take a stroll around the district to admire the street art and unique architecture. Maboneng is known for its urban renewal and the area is filled with interesting murals and renovated industrial buildings. You can also spend the afternoon exploring the Maboneng Precinct with a Guided Bicycle Tour with Lunch for US$ 37.17. This revitalized district is known for its street art, boutiques, and galleries. Do not miss the Arts on Main, a

multi-purpose space that houses artist studios, galleries, and shops.

Late afternoon: Rooftop Bar
End your tour at one of Maboneng's rooftop bars, such as The Living m, where you can enjoy a drink with a view of the city.

Please note that this is a suggested itinerary, and the exact route and schedule might vary depending on your personal preferences and the operating hours of each site. Always check the latest information directly with the attractions and consider your safety when choosing transportation methods.

10 5 -Day Itinerary to Pilanesberg

Should you have extra time in Johannesburg, it is worthwhile extending the 3-day trip into a 5-day trip that can include the Pilanesberg National Park.

A summary of the 5-day itinerary is:
Day 1: Soweto, Hector Pietersen Museum, Apartheid Museum, and Constitution Hill with lunch in Soweto
Day 2: A tour of the Maboneng district, visit to the Museum of African Design, lunch at Pata Pata or another local restaurant, and the afternoon doing a bicycle tour of the area.
Day 3: Depart from Johannesburg for Sun City and Pilanesberg. Explore Sun City and overnight at Sun City.
Day 4: Day trip to the Pilanesberg National Park. Evening enjoy the entertainment and restaurants in Sun City.
Day 5: Spend the morning exploring the outdoor activities at Sun City. Depart from Sun City in the afternoon.

Day 1: Explore Johannesburg's History and Culture

Interactive Map of the Directions for Day 1 trip(https://bit.ly/3NF7tDA)

Morning: Start with Soweto
Begin your day early by taking a taxi or Uber from you accommodation in Johannesburg to Soweto. Aim to leave by 8:00 AM to make the most of your day.

First Stop: Hector Pieterson Museum
Your first stop in Soweto should be the *Hector Pieterson Museum*. This museum is dedicated to the 1976 uprising in Soweto and th tragic death of Hector Pieterson, a 12-year-old boy who became symbol of the struggle against apartheid. The museum opens a 10:00 AM.

Second Stop: Vilakazi Street
Next, head to *Vilakazi Street*, the only street in the world that ha been home to two Nobel Peace Prize laureates - Nelson Mandela an Desmond Tutu. Here you can visit the *Mandela House Museum*, whic was once the residence of Nelson Mandela.

Lunch in Soweto
After exploring Vilakazi Street, grab lunch at a local restauran *Sakhumzi Restaurant* is a popular spot that serves traditional Sout African cuisine.

Afternoon: Apartheid Museum
After lunch, take a taxi or Uber to the *Apartheid Museum*, which i about a 30-minute drive from Soweto. This museum offers an in depth look at the history of apartheid through a series of powerfu

exhibits. Plan to spend at least a couple of hours here to fully explore the museum.

Evening: Constitution Hill
From the Apartheid Museum, take a taxi or Uber to *Constitution Hill*, a former prison complex that now houses the Constitutional Court. Here you can learn about South Africa's journey to democracy. The site closes at 5:00 PM, so aim to get there by 3:00 PM to give yourself enough time to explore.

After your visit to Constitution Hill, you can take a taxi or Uber back to your accommodation in Johannesburg.

Please note that this is a suggested itinerary and the times, order of attractions, and transportation methods may need to be adjusted based on your personal preferences, the location of your accommodation, and the operating hours of each site. Always check the latest information directly with the attractions and consider your safety when choosing transportation methods.

Day 2: Self-guided tour of the Maboneng District

Interactive May of Day 2: Self-guided tour of the Maboneng District(https://bit.ly/3Xkx1cz)

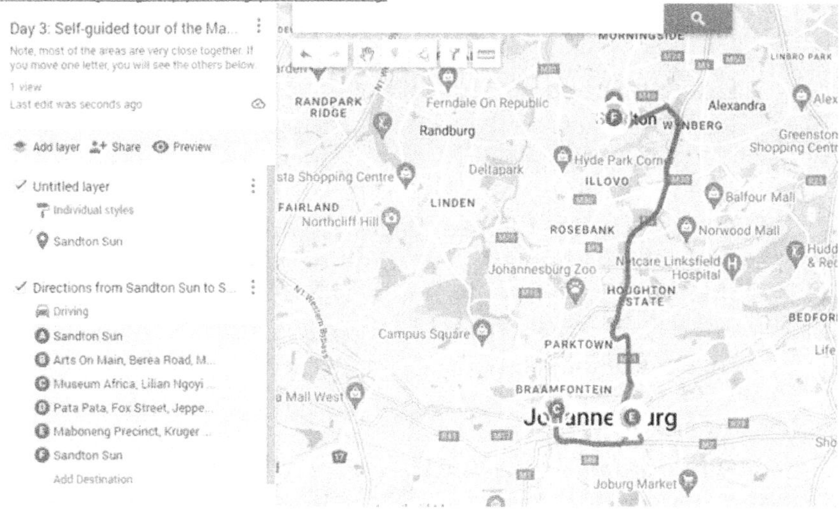

Morning: Start at Arts on Main

Begin your tour at Arts on Main, a vibrant arts precinct in the Maboneng district. Here, you can explore various art galleries, artist studios, and craft shops. The area also hosts a popular market on Sundays.

Next: MOAD (Museum of African Design)
From Arts on Main, take a short walk to the Museum of African Design (MOAD). This is the first museum in Africa dedicated to design. MOAD hosts a variety of exhibitions and events throughout the year.

Lunch: Local Restaurants
For lunch, there are numerous restaurants and cafes in the Maboneng district offering a variety of cuisines. Pata Pata is a popular spot known for its African dishes.

Afternoon: Street Art and Architecture
After lunch, take a stroll around the district to admire the street art and unique architecture. Maboneng is known for its urban renewal and the area is filled with interesting murals and renovated industrial buildings. You can also spend the afternoon exploring the Maboneng Precinct with a Guided Bicycle Tour with Lunch for US$ 37.17. This revitalized district is known for its street art, boutiques, and galleries. Do not miss the Arts on Main, a multi-purpose space that houses artist studios, galleries, and shops.

Late afternoon: Rooftop Bar
End your tour at one of Maboneng's rooftop bars, such as The Living m, where you can enjoy a drink with a view of the city.

Please note that this is a suggested itinerary, and the exact route and schedule might vary depending on your personal preferences and the operating hours of each site. Always check the latest information directly with the attractions and consider your safety when choosing transportation methods.

Day 3: Pilanesberg and Sun City

Day 3: Map from Sandton to Sun City and Pilanesberg

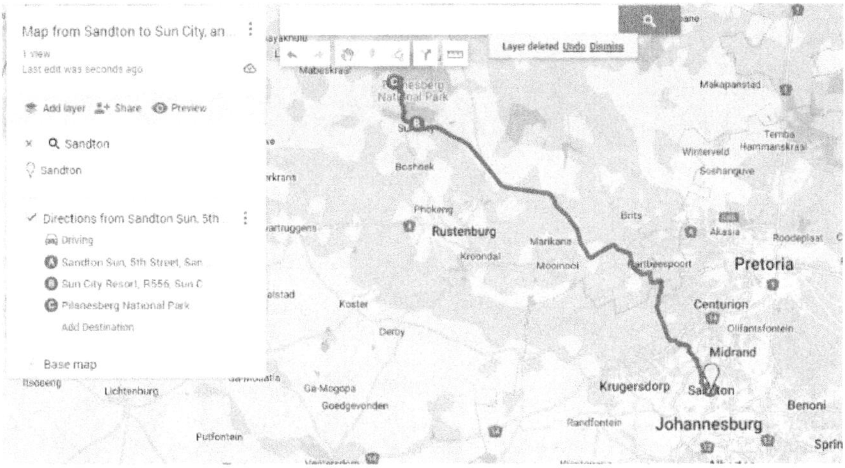

Depart from Johannesburg in the morning. The drive to Sun City is approximately 2 hours. Upon arrival, check into your hotel. I recommend *The Cabanas Hotel at Sun City Resort*. This family-friendly hotel is conveniently located near the airport and within walking distance of Waterworld and Sun City Casino. The hotel offers a full-service spa, a golf course, a casino, free water park access, and an outdoor pool. The average nightly price is $149.01.

Spend the rest of the day exploring Sun City. You can enjoy the water park, try your luck at the casino, or relax at the spa. For dinner, there are 10 restaurants at the hotel to choose from.

Day 4: Visit to Pilanesberg

On the second day, take a day trip to Pilanesberg National Park. The park is about a 30-minute drive from Sun City. Spend the day on a self-guided safari, spotting wildlife and enjoying the beautiful scenery.

Map from Sun City Resort to Pilanesberg National Park(https://bit.ly/3qMWFua)

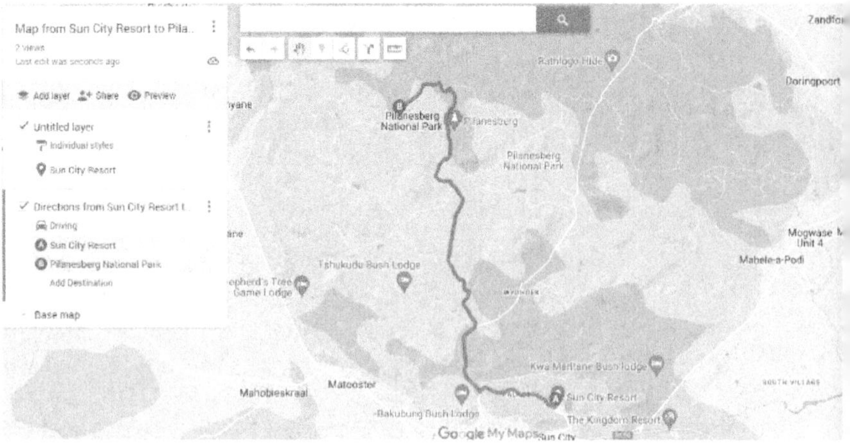

Information regarding entering and driving in Pilanesberg National Park

Pilanesberg National Park is a popular destination in South Africa known for its rich wildlife and beautiful landscapes. Here are some general guidelines for entering the park and self-driving:

Entrance Procedure: Upon arrival at the park, you will need to pay an entrance fee at the gate. The fee varies depending on the season and the age of the visitors. It's advisable to check the latest fees on the official website before your visit. You'll receive a permit which you should keep with you at all times during your visit.

Park Hours: The park is open throughout the year. However, the opening and closing times vary depending on the season. It's usually open from sunrise to sunset. Make sure to check the exact timings prior to your visit.

Self-Driving Rules: Self-drive safaris are a popular way to explore Pilanesberg National Park. Here are some rules to follow:

- Stick to the speed limit: The speed limit is usually 40km/h on tarred roads and 20km/h on gravel roads.
- Stay on the roads: Off-road driving is strictly prohibited as it can damage the ecosystem and disturb the wildlife.
- Do not get out of your vehicle: Except in designated areas, do not get out of your vehicle for your safety and the well-being of the animals.
- Keep a safe distance: Maintain a safe distance from the animals. Do not try to feed or touch them.

- Keep quiet: Noise can disturb the animals. Keep the noise level to a minimum.
- No pets: Pets are not allowed in the park.

Remember, the aim is to observe and appreciate the wildlife in their natural habitat without disturbing them. Always respect the rules and regulations of the park to ensure a safe and enjoyable visit for you and the other visitors.

Please note that the information provided here is general advice and the specific rules and procedures may vary. Always check the latest information from the official website or directly contact the park authorities before your visit.

For lunch, pack a picnic to enjoy in the park. Return to Sun City in the late afternoon and enjoy dinner at one of the resort's restaurants.

Day 5: More Sun City and Departure

Spend the morning enjoying more of what Sun City has to offer. You could play a round of golf, relax by the pool, or explore more of the resort.

Check out of your hotel and begin the drive back to Johannesburg in the afternoon.

Please note that this is a suggested itinerary, and the exact schedule might vary depending on your personal preferences and the operating hours of each site. Always check the latest information directly with the attractions and consider your safety when choosing transportation methods.

11 10-Day Itinerary in the Kruger National Park

For a full experience of Johannesburg and Mpumalanga, plan a 10-day trip to include some of the attractions in Mpumalanga and spend 3 days in the Kruger National Park.

A summary of this 10-day itinerary:
Day 1: Tour of Soweto, Apartheid Museum, and Constitution Hill.

Day 2: A day trip to Sun City and Pilanesberg
Day 3: A day trip to the Maboneng District
Day 4: Departure to Mpumalanga
Day 5: Overnight at Pilgrims Rest
Day 6: Overnight in Graskop
Day 7 – Day 9: Kruger National Park
Day 10: Travel back to Johannesburg

Day 1: Explore Johannesburg's History and Culture

Book a full-day guided tour to visit Soweto, Apartheid Museum, and Constitution Hill.

Suggested Tour Companies

- Get your Guide
- MoAfrika Tours
- Stephenson Adventures

Interactive Map of the Directions for Day 1: Exploring Culture

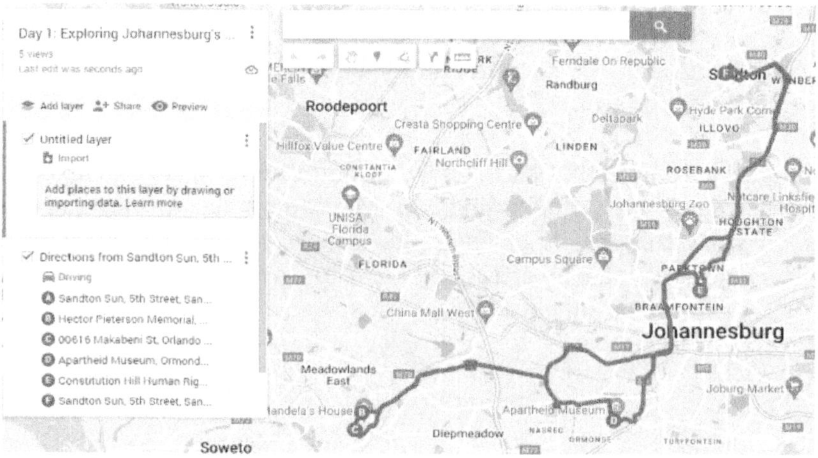

Morning
This tour typically starts in the morning around 8:00 AM. You will b picked up from your hotel in Johannesburg and driven to Sowet (South Western Townships), which is about a 30-minute drive.

First Stop: Soweto

In Soweto, you will visit the Hector Pieterson Museum, dedicated to a 12-year-old boy who was one of the first casualties of the Soweto uprising in 1976. You will learn about the events leading up to this tragic event and its aftermath.

Next, you will visit Vilakazi Street, the only street in the world that has been home to two Nobel Peace Prize laureates - Nelson Mandela and Desmond Tutu. You can see the former home of Nelson Mandela, which is now the Mandela House Museum.

Lunch in Soweto
After exploring Soweto, you will have lunch at a local restaurant where you can try traditional South African cuisine.

Second Stop: Apartheid Museum
After lunch, you will be driven to the *Apartheid Museum*, which is about a 30-minute drive from Soweto. Here, you will learn about the history of apartheid through a series of powerful exhibits. The museum tells the story of apartheid from its inception, its development, and its demise with the election of Nelson Mandela as South Africa's first black president.

The tour typically ends around 5:00 PM, and you will be driven back to your hotel in Johannesburg.

Day 2: Tour to Pilanesberg Nature Reserve

This full-day safari tour takes you from Johannesburg to the Pilanesberg Nature Reserve.

Suggested Tour Companies where you can book a tour:

- Get your Guide
- MoAfrika Tours
- Stephenson Adventures

Here's a detailed itinerary:

Interactive map of Day 2: Day Trip to Pilanesberg

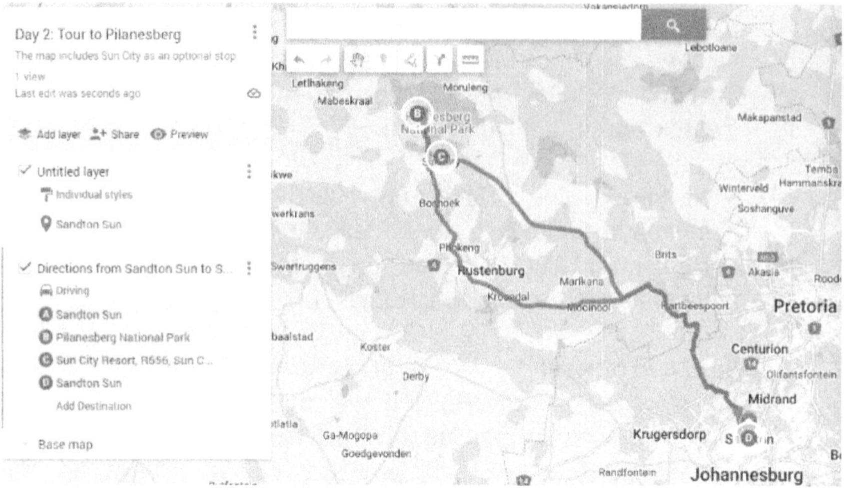

Morning: Departure from Johannesburg

The tour departs from Johannesburg early in the morning. You will be picked up from your hotel by the tour company. The tour operator will confirm the exact time of departure, but it's typically around 6:00 AM.

Arrival at Pilanesberg Nature Reserve

After a drive of approximately 2.5 hours, you will arrive at the Pilanesberg Nature Reserve. Here, you will join a ranger in an open vehicle for a game drive.

Game Drive in Pilanesberg Nature Reserve

During the game drive, you will have the opportunity to see a variety of wildlife, including lions, giraffes, cheetahs, hippos, and crocodiles. The ranger will provide insightful commentary about the animals and their natural habitat.

Lunch in the Park

Lunch is typically included in these types of tours, but the specifics will depend on the tour operator. You might have lunch at one of the rest camps in the park.

Afternoon: Continue Game Drive

After lunch, you will continue your game drive in the park. This is a great time to spot more wildlife and take in the beautiful scenery of the park.

Evening: Return to Johannesburg

In the late afternoon, you will begin your journey back to Johannesburg. You should arrive back at your hotel in the evening.

The cost of the tour typically includes transportation, a guide, entrance fees to the park, and lunch. However, it's always a good idea to check the latest information directly with the tour provider. The starting price for this tour is approximately US$ 155.84 per person.

Please note that the exact route and schedule might vary depending on the tour provider.

Day 3: Self-guided tour of the Maboneng District

Interactive May of Day 3: Self-guided tour of the Maboneng District

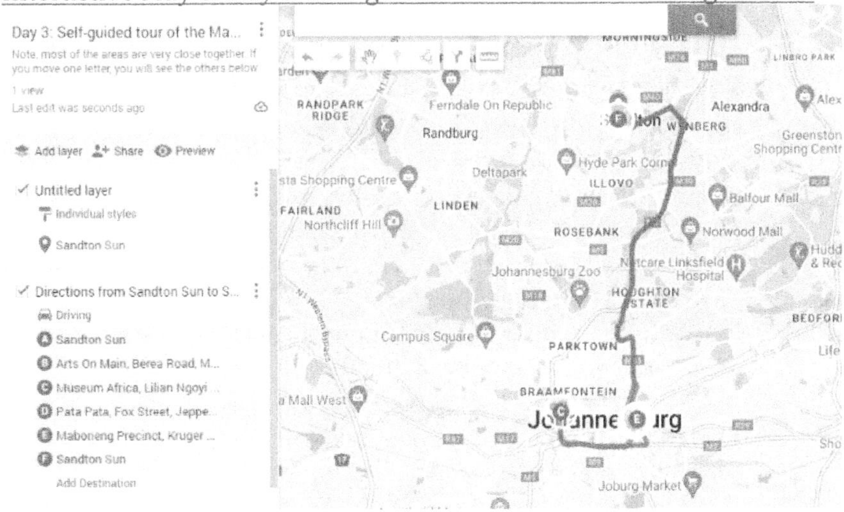

Morning: Start at Arts on Main

Begin your tour at Arts on Main, a vibrant arts precinct in the Maboneng district. Here, you can explore various art galleries, artist studios, and craft shops. The area also hosts a popular market on Sundays.

Next: MOAD (Museum of African Design)

From Arts on Main, take a short walk to the Museum of African Design (MOAD). This is the first museum in Africa dedicated to design. MOAD hosts a variety of exhibitions and events throughout the year.

Lunch: Local Restaurants

For lunch, there are numerous restaurants and cafes in the Maboneng district offering a variety of cuisines. Pata Pata is a popular spot known for its African dishes.

Afternoon: Street Art and Architecture

After lunch, take a stroll around the district to admire the street art and unique architecture. Maboneng is known for its urban renewal and the area is filled with interesting murals and renovated industrial buildings. You can also spend the afternoon exploring the Maboneng Precinct with a Guided Bicycle Tour with Lunch for US$ 37.17. This revitalized district is known for its street art, boutiques, and galleries. Do not miss the Arts on Main, a multi-purpose space that houses artist studios, galleries, and shops.

Late afternoon: Rooftop Bar

End your tour at one of Maboneng's rooftop bars, such as The Living m, where you can enjoy a drink with a view of the city.

Please note that this is a suggested itinerary, and the exact route and schedule might vary depending on your personal preferences and the operating hours of each site. Always check the latest information directly with the attractions and consider your safety when choosing transportation methods.

Day 4: Travel from Johannesburg to Mbombela in Mpumalanga

Depart from Johannesburg by 08:00am to Mbombela (Nelspruit) in Mpumalanga. Take the N12 and N4. The journey is approximately 220 miles which should take around 4 hours.

Map from Sandton to Mbombela in Mpumalanga

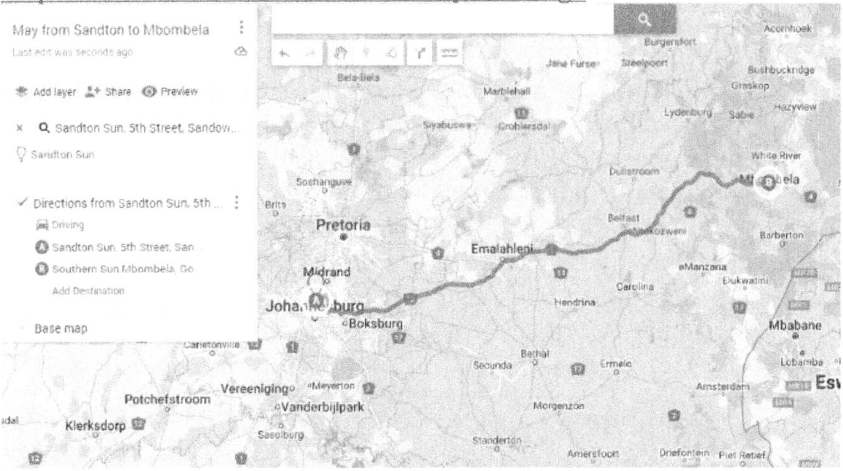

You can stay at one of the following hotels in Mbombela:

Southern Sun Mbombela

The hotel is located at 15 Government Boulevard, Riverside Park Ext 1, in Nelspruit. Part of the Southern Sun Hotel Group, you can expect a choice of well-appointed rooms from standard rooms to executive rooms. The rates include uncapped Wi-fi, DStv, tea/ coffee facilities, and breakfast. Two children under 18 may stay for free when

sharing when an adult. The room rates are from US$98, subject t change.
For more information or to book a room please visit Southern Su Mbombela.

Protea Hotel by Marriott Nelspruit
Protea Hotel by Marriott Nelspruit is situated at 30 Jerepico Street, Orchards, Mbombela. This is an award-winning hotel located on 40 miles from the Kruger National Park, is an ideal destination to explore the natural attractions of Mpumalanga before moving onto the Kruger National Park. All rooms offer uncapped Wi-Fi, satellite TV, electronic safes, and coffee/ tea maker. The room rates are from US$90, subject to change.
For more information or to book a room please visit Protea Hotel by Marriot Nelspruit

Day 5: Exploring God's Window, Blyde River Canyon, Berlin Falls and Lisbon Falls

Book a full day tour to take you to all the main attractions i Mpumalanga. The tour will take you to the attractions detaile below.

The entrance fee to the attractions is included in the tour price.

Tours can be booked at any of the following tour companies:

- Mbombela Experience Tours and Safaris (https://www.mbombelatours.com/)
- Get Your Guide(https://bit.ly/3CLTbuB)
- Detour Africa(https://bit.ly/3CF80PL)

For interest sake, the map below indicates where all the attractions are located in Mpumalanga.

Map showing the location of the tourist attractions in Mpumalanga(https://bit.ly/44deNvE)

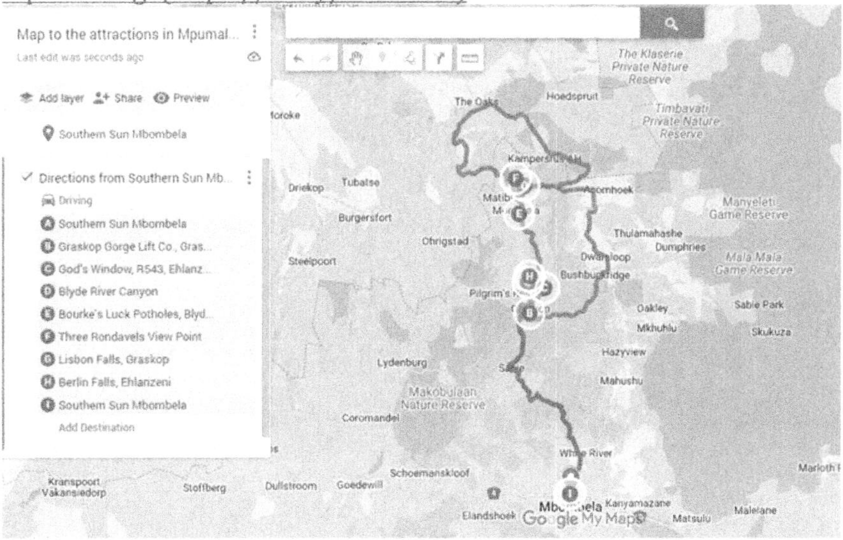

The Gorge Lift

The Graskop Gorge Lift is an exciting and innovative tourism development in the heart of South Africa's Panorama Route in Mpumalanga. The lift takes visitors 51 meters down the face of the gorge into the forest below, where wooden walkways and suspension bridges meander along a 600 meter trail through the indigenous forest with interactive exhibits.

The Graskop Gorge Lift is the first viewing elevator of its kind in Africa and offers a unique and thrilling perspective on the Graskop Gorge and the forest ecosystem below. The journey down into the gorge is a thrilling experience as the circular viewing platform slowly descends, offering panoramic views of the waterfall and the lush forest.

At the bottom of the gorge, visitors can explore the forest along a wooden walkway, which includes interactive exhibits, beautiful waterfalls, and abundant birdlife. The gorge is home to a number of species of birds, including the elusive Narina Trogon and the African Finfoot.

For more information regarding the variety of activities and ticket prices visit Gorge Lift. (https://www.graskopgorgeliftcompany.co.za/rates.html)

God's Window

God's Window is one of the most popular and scenic vantage points in South Africa. It's located along the Drakensberg escarpment in Mpumalanga, and it's part of the Blyde River Canyon Nature Reserve. From God's Window, visitors are treated to a stunning panoramic view of cliffs dropping over 700 meters down into lush, indigenous forest-clad ravine, the green Lowveld, and beyond to the Kruger National Park and Mozambique. On a clear day, it's possible to see over the Kruger National Park towards the Lebombo Mountains on the border of Mozambique.

God's Window is so called because the panoramic view it offers of the Lowveld more than 900 meters down into lush indigenous forest-clad ravine is said to be God's window onto the world. The reserve is also home to a diversity of plants and wildlife, including over 300 species of birds.

Blyde River Canyon:

The Blyde River Canyon is one of the largest canyons on Earth, and arguably the most beautiful. It is located in the Mpumalanga province of South Africa and is part of the Drakensberg escarpment. The canyon stretches over 25 kilometers and is 750 meters deep on average.

The Blyde River Canyon is known for its breathtaking panoramic views and diverse flora and fauna. It is home to numerous species of wildlife, including hippos, antelopes, and primates. The canyon is also rich in birdlife, making it a popular destination for bird watching.

The canyon offers several viewpoints, including the famous God's Window, which provides stunning views of the canyon and the Lowveld below. Other notable viewpoints include Bourke's Luck Potholes, a series of natural geological formations that offer a unique view of the canyon's rock layers, and the Three Rondavels, massive round rocks that resemble traditional African huts.

The Blyde River Canyon is also a hub for adventure activities. Visitors can enjoy hiking, horse riding, white-water rafting, hot-air ballooning, and fly-fishing. There are also several beautiful waterfalls in the area, including the Lisbon Falls and Berlin Falls.

Bourke's Luck Potholes

Bourke's Luck Potholes are a natural water feature and a major tourist attraction in South Africa. They are located at the confluence of the Treur River and Blyde River in the Blyde River Canyon Nature Reserve in Mpumalanga. The potholes were formed by centuries of water erosion and the swirling whirlpools which occur as the Treur River plunges into the Blyde River causing waterborne sand and rock to grind deep, cylindrical potholes into the bedrock of the river.

The result is a series of cylindrical rock sculptures that are a testament to the power of water in a landscape. The potholes are named after a gold digger, Tom Bourke, who predicted the presence of gold, though he found none himself.
The area offers beautiful views, hiking trails, and picnic spots. It's also near to other attractions on the Panorama Route, such as God's Window and the Three Rondavels.

Three Rondavels

The Three Rondavels are a famous geological formation locate within the Blyde River Canyon Nature Reserve in Mpumalang South Africa. They are three round, grass-covered mountain top with slightly pointed tops, very similar to the traditional round c oval African homesteads known as rondavels.

The Three Rondavels are named after the three most troublesom wives of Chief Maripi Mashile - they are Magabolle, Mogoladikw and Maseroto. The view point provides a breathtaking view over th Blyde River Canyon and the Three Rondavels.

Lisbon Waterfalls

Lisbon Falls is one of the most dramatic waterfalls in the area and is named after the capital city of Portugal. It is the highest waterfall in Mpumalanga, South Africa, with a drop of 94 meters. The waterfall is located near the town of Graskop and is a popular tourist attraction. The waterfall is surrounded by lush vegetation and offers a beautiful view, especially after heavy rainfall when the water cascades down the cliff in a spectacular display.

Berlin Falls

Berlin Falls is another popular waterfall in the area. It's named after the German city of Berlin. The waterfall is about eighty meters high, and the river plunges into a circular basin, creating a beautiful and dramatic scene. The waterfall is surrounded by a lush green landscape and is a great spot for picnicking and photography.

Day 6: Explore Nelspruit

Interactive map for exploring Mbombela (https://bit.ly/42SGkkY)

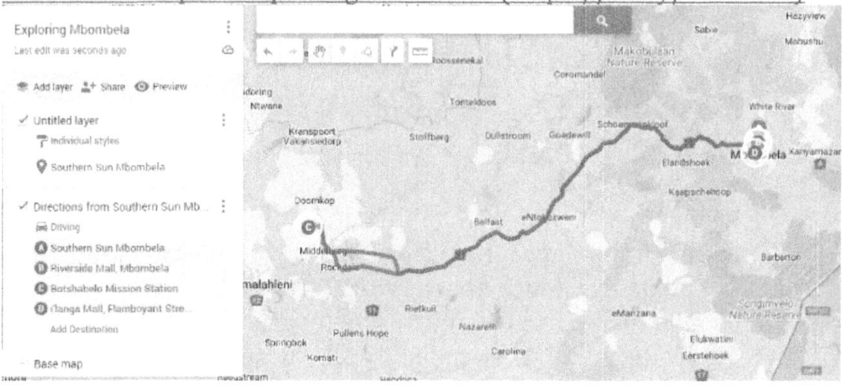

Morning
Have a leisurely breakfast at the hotel. Then head to into the city.

Shopping in Nelspruit: Nelspruit offers a variety of shopping experiences. The Riverside Mall and Ilanga Mall are two of the biggest shopping centers in the city, offering a wide range of stores, from fashion to electronics, as well as restaurants and cinemas. The city is also home to several markets, including the Halls Gateway Market, which offers a variety of local products, from fresh produce to handmade crafts.

Lunch
Enjoy lunch in one of the restaurants in the city.

Afternoon
Spend the afternoon exploring the cultural experiences of Nelspruit. Nelspruit is rich in cultural heritage. Spend time experiencing the Mpumalanga Cultural & Heritage Route. The route includes the

Botshabelo Mission Station, an open-air museum that showcases traditional Ndebele art.

Evening

Spend the evening at the Emnotweni Casino offers a taste of the city's nightlife. Enjoy dinner in one of their restaurants.

Map from Southern Sun Mbombela to the Emnotweni Casino(https://bit.ly/46rYgpQ)

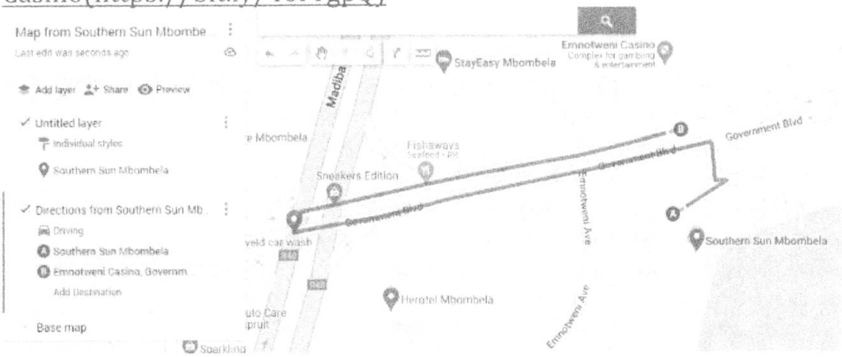

Day 7: Kruger National Park

Morning

Depart from the hotel and head towards Hazyview and the Paul Kruger Gate, one of the main entry points to the Kruger National Park. The trip is about seventy miles and should take between an hour and a half and two hours.

Interactive map with directions from Southern Sun Mbombela to the Paul Kruger Entrance Gate(https://bit.ly/3Jm9uSI)

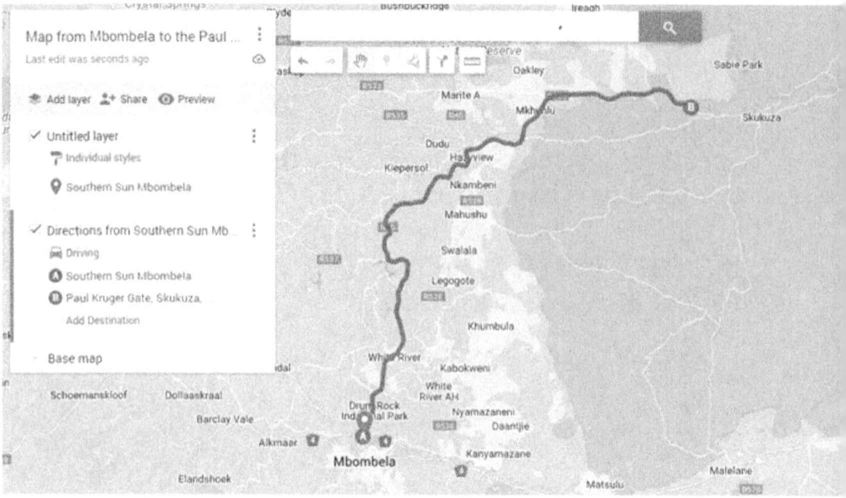

Accommodation in Kruger National Park

During your stay at the Kruger National Park, you have a variety of options for accommodation. You can select between the rest camps in the Kruger National Park, or Private Lodges within the Kruger Park.

Booking accommodation for the rest camps in the Kruger National Park must be done well in advance. The website for bookings is Kruger National Park.

Some suggestions for accommodation for three days in the Kruger National Park, include two nights at Satara Rest Camp and one night at Lower Sabie Rest Camp.

When entering the Kruger National Park through the Paul Kruger Gate, tourists need to follow a certain procedure to ensure a smooth entry. Here is a step-by-step guide:

Arrival at the Gate: Upon arrival at the Paul Kruger Gate, you will be required to stop at the entrance. There are usually park officials present to guide you through the process.

Vehicle Inspection: Park officials may conduct a brief inspection of your vehicle. This is a routine procedure to ensure that no illegal substances or activities are being carried into the park.

Entry Fee Payment: You will be required to pay an entry fee at the gate. The fee varies depending on the nationality of the visitor (South African citizens get a discount). The standard conservation fee for international visitors is approximately US$26 for adults and US$13 for children. You will be given a map of the park.

Filling Out a Registration Form: You will need to fill out a registration form with details such as your name, number of people in the vehicle, vehicle registration, and intended duration of stay. This is for record-keeping and safety purposes.

Receiving a Permit: Once the form is filled out and the fee is paid, you will receive a permit. This permit must be kept with you at all times during your stay in the park and shown at all rest camps and when exiting the park.

Park Regulations Briefing: Park officials will provide you with a brief overview of the park rules and regulations. These include speed limits (50 km/h on tar roads, 40 km/h on gravel), prohibition of feeding animals, staying inside your vehicle, and sticking to designated roads and paths.

Entry into the Park: Once all the formalities are completed, you will be allowed to enter the park. The gate opening and closing times vary depending on the time of year, so make sure you plan your arrival accordingly to avoid being denied entry.

Remember, the Kruger National Park is a protected area and home to a vast array of wildlife. It is important to respect all rules and regulations to ensure the safety and well-being of the animals and the enjoyment of all visitors. Enjoy your visit to this magnificent park!

The map below shows the various rest camps in the Kruger National Park.

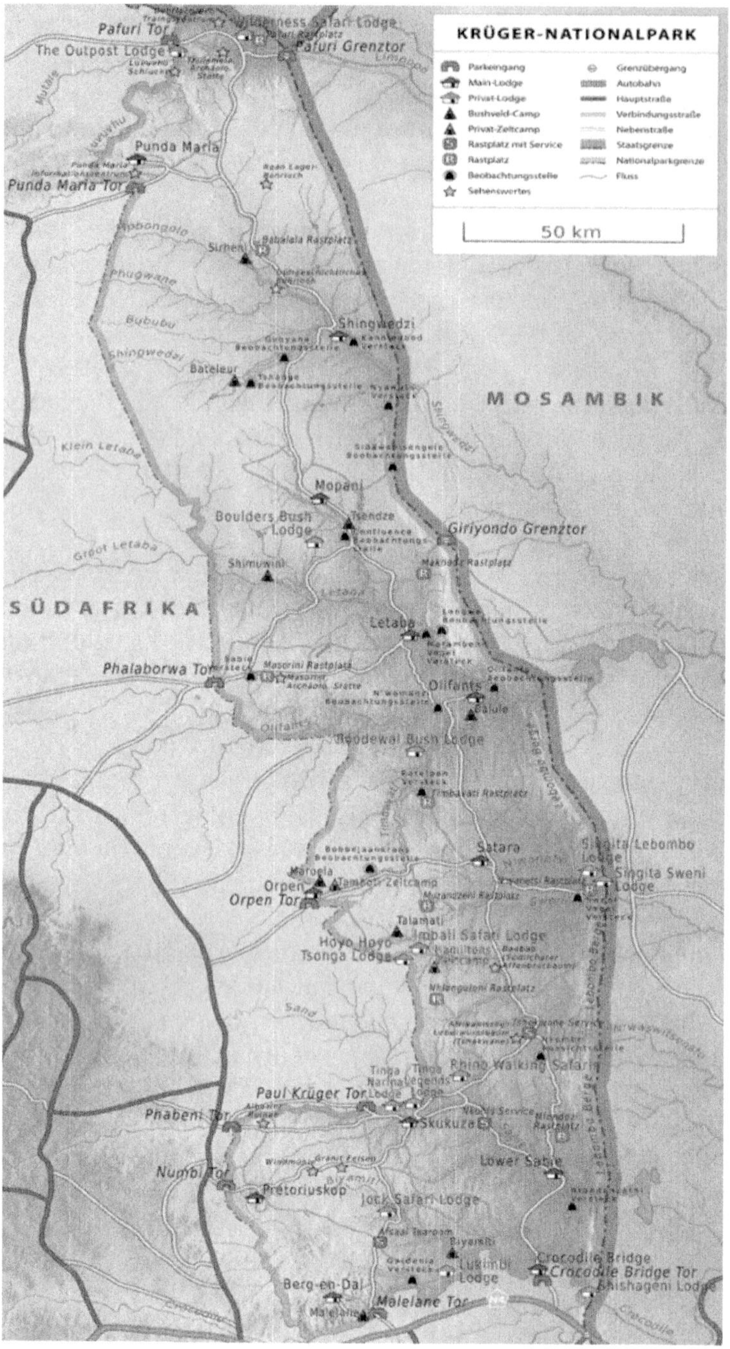
KRÜGER-NATIONALPARK
Parkeingang
Main-Lodge
Privat-Lodge
Bushveld-Camp
Privat-Zeltcamp
Rastplatz mit Service
Rastplatz
Beobachtungsstelle
Sehenswertes
Grenzübergang
Autobahn
Hauptstraße
Verbindungsstraße
Nebenstraße
Staatsgrenze
Nationalparkgrenze
Fluss
50 km
MOSAMBIK
SÜDAFRIKA
Pafuri Tor
The Outpost Lodge
Pafuri Grenztor
Punda Maria
Punda Maria Tor
Sirheni
Babalala Rastplatz
Shingwedzi
Bateleur
Mopani
Boulders Bush Lodge
Tsendze
Shimuwini
Giriyondo Grenztor
Letaba
Phalaborwa Tor
Masorini Rastplatz
Olifants
Balule
Roodewal Bush Lodge
Timbavati Rastplatz
Satara
Singita Lebombo Lodge
Singita Sweni Lodge
Maroela
Orpen
Orpen Tor
Tamboti Zeltcamp
Talamati
Imbali Safari Lodge
Hoyo Hoyo Tsonga Lodge
Nhlanguleni Rastplatz
Rhino Walking Safaris
Tinga Narina Lodge
Tinga Legends Lodge
Paul Krüger Tor
Phabeni Tor
Skukuza
Lower Sabie
Numbi Tor
Pretoriuskop
Jock Safari Lodge
Biyamiti
Lukimbi Lodge
Crocodile Bridge
Crocodile Bridge Tor
Shishangeni Lodge
Berg-en-Dal
Malelane Tor
Malelane
Limpopo
Mutale
Luvuvhu
Mphongolo
Phugwane
Bububu
Shingwedzi
Klein Letaba
Groot Letaba
Letaba
Olifants
Sand
Sabie
Crocodile
Lebombo Berge

After entry to the park make your way to the first rest camp, Skukuza. This is the biggest rest camp in the Kruger National Park. It hosts a small airfield therefore it is possible to fly into the Kruger National Park and rent a vehicle from the Skukuza Rest Camp.

You can stock up on food items at the shop, although all the camps do have shops where you can buy basic ingredients. After browsing through the rest camp make your way to Satara Rest Camp. Although the distance is not far, only 58 miles, the journey will take a minimum of 2 hours. Remember the speed limit is 40km/h on gravel roads and 50 km/h on tar roads. The point of traveling through the Kruger National Park is to drive slowly to find animals. You also never know when you will come across a siting where you want to sit a while to enjoy the experience.

The rest camps have specific opening and closing times depending on the time of year. These times are:

Opening times:

- Oct: 05:30
- Nov - Jan: 04:30
- Feb - Mar: 05:30
- Apr - Sep: 06:00

Closing times:

- Aug - Oct: 18:00
- Nov - Feb: 18:30
- Mar - Apr: 18:00
- May - Jul: 17:30

When staying at a rest camp in the Kruger National Park, tourists have several options for meals. Here are some of the options:

Self-Catering: Most accommodation units in the rest camps come equipped with a braai (barbecue) facility. You can bring your own food and cook it on the braai. This is a popular option as it allows you to enjoy a traditional South African braai under the stars. You will need to bring your own charcoal or wood, as well as braai utensils. Some units also have kitchen facilities where you can prepare meals.

Camp Restaurants: Most of the larger rest camps have restaurants where you can enjoy a meal. These restaurants usually offer a variety of options, from traditional South African cuisine to more international dishes. It's a good idea to check the opening hours as they can vary between camps.

Picnic Sites: There are also designated picnic sites in the park where you can enjoy a meal in the great outdoors. These sites usually have braai facilities and sometimes even a small shop where you can buy basic supplies.

Camp Shops: All rest camps have shops where you can buy groceries, including meat for the braai, as well as other essentials like bread, milk, and canned goods. Some also sell ready-made meals that you can heat up in your accommodation.

Remember, it is important to store food securely to avoid attracting animals, and never feed the wildlife. Enjoy your meals in the beautiful setting of the Kruger National Park!

Day 8: Plan daily trips around the Kruger National Park

Over the next two days plan daily excursions in the Kruger National Park for viewing animals and experiencing the environment. Here is a guideline how you can plan a trip for the day in the Kruger National Park. Use the Kruger National Park map to plan your own individual trip.

Morning Wake-Up

Your day in the Kruger National Park should start early, ideally just before the gates open. This is because many animals are most active during the cooler hours of the early morning. Wake up, freshen up, and grab a quick breakfast or pack something to eat on the go.

Early Morning Game Drive

As soon as the camp gates open (times vary depending on the season, so check the exact times), head out for your morning game drive. The early morning is a great time to spot predators like lions, leopards, and hyenas, as they are often still active from their night-time hunts.

The best roads for game viewing can depend on recent sightings and animal movements, which can be unpredictable. However, the roads around Lower Sabie, Satara, and Crocodile Bridge rest camps are known for good game viewing. The S100 road near Satara, in particular, has a reputation for lion and cheetah sightings.

Mid-Morning Break
After a few hours of game viewing, find a nice picnic spot or return to your rest camp for a mid-morning break. You can have a snack, rest, and plan your next drive.

Mid-Day Activities
During the heat of the day, animals are often less active and may be harder to spot. This is a good time to visit one of the park's visitor centers or museums, like the Letaba Elephant Museum or the Albasini Ruins near Phabeni Gate. Alternatively, you could attend a ranger talk if one is available, or simply relax at your rest camp.

Afternoon Game Drive
In the late afternoon, as the day starts to cool down, head out for another game drive. Animals start to become more active again during this time. The area around the Olifants rest camp is great for elephant sightings, while the road between Lower Sabie and Skukuza is known for its high density of leopards.

Evening Return to Camp
Make sure you return to your rest camp before the gates close (again, times vary depending on the season). You could have a braai (barbecue) for dinner, a common tradition in South Africa, or dine at the camp's restaurant if one is available.

Remember, the key to a successful day in the Kruger National Park is patience and keeping your eyes open for any signs of animal activity. Enjoy your day in this magnificent park!

Day 9: Plan daily including departure from Satara Rest Camp and traveling to Lower Sabie Rest Camp

The previous evening plan, the trip you will be taking from the Satara Rest Camp to the Lower Sabie Rest Camp. Use the Kruger National Park map to plan your own individual route to the Lower Sabie Rest Camp.

Early morning

Wake up early, pack and be ready to leave the Satara Rest Camp by the time the gates open. Follow your route until you reach the Lower Sabie Rest Camp, remember you cannot check in before 2:00PM on the day of your arrival. The direct route from Satara to Lower Sabie is approximately sixty miles and will take 2 hours without any stoppages.

Mid-Morning Break

After a few hours of game viewing, find a nice picnic spot or return to your rest camp for a mid-morning break. You can have a snack, rest, and plan your next drive. There are two popular rest camps between Satara and Lower Sabie Rest Camps called Tshokwane Picnic Site and Nkuhlu Picnic Site.

Afternoon Activities

Arrive at Lower Sabie by 3:00PM. Check into your rondavel, and settle in. You can plan a late afternoon game drive in the area surrounding Lower Sabie.

Evening Return to Camp

Make sure you return to your rest camp before the gates close (again, times vary depending on the season). You could have a braai (barbecue) for dinner, a common tradition in South Africa, or dine at the camp's restaurant,

Day 10: Check out of Lower Sabie and return to Johannesburg

Morning Wake-Up

Your day in the Kruger National Park should start early, ideally just before the gates open. This is because many animals are most active during the cooler hours of the early morning. Wake up, freshen up, and grab a quick breakfast or pack something to eat on the go.

Early Morning Game Drive

As soon as the camp gates open (times vary depending on the season, so check the exact times), head out for your final morning game drive in the area surrounding Lower Sabie. Be sure to be back at the rest camp by 09:30AM as check-out time is 10:00AM.

Mid-Morning
After checking out of your rondavel at Lower Sabie, head towards Skukuza and the Paul Kruger Gate. The trip between Lower Sabie and the Kruger Gate is about 36 miles and will take an hour and a half without any stoppages.

Enjoy your final game drive through the Kruger National Park as you head to the Paul Kruger Gate where you can exit the park. Make sure to reach this gate by 1:00PM at the latest as the drive back to Johannesburg is approximately 5 hours and it is better to not travel at night.

Tips for a Memorable Experience in the Kruger National Park

Early Morning and Late Afternoon Game Drives: The best times to spot wildlife are during the cooler parts of the day, early in the morning and late in the afternoon. Animals are most active during these times, and you're more likely to see them out and about.

Pack Binoculars and a Camera: Binoculars are essential for spotting wildlife at a distance, and a good camera will help you capture those unforgettable moments.

Stay Quiet: Noise can scare off animals. When you're on a game drive, try to stay as quiet as possible to increase your chances of seeing wildlife.

Respect the Animals: Remember that you are in their home. Keep a safe distance, do not feed the animals, and never get out of your vehicle unless in a designated area.

Dress Appropriately: Wear neutral colors that blend in with the bush, and remember to pack a hat, sunglasses, and sunscreen. Even in winter, the African sun can be strong.

Stay Hydrated and Pack Snacks: Game drives can be long, and you might not have access to food or water. Always bring water and some snacks with you.

Use a Map: The Kruger National Park is vast. A map will help you understand where you are and plan your route for the day. They are available at the entrance gates and rest camps.

Patience is Key: Wildlife spotting requires patience. You might no see anything for a while and then suddenly come across a pride o lions. Enjoy the quiet moments and keep your eyes peeled.

Guided Tours: Consider booking a guided tour, especially if it i your first visit. Guides are experienced and knowledgeable, and the can enhance your experience by providing interesting informatio about the animals and the park.

Malaria Precautions: The Kruger National Park is in a malaria zone Consult with your doctor about taking malaria prophylaxis an remember to pack insect repellent.

Remember, every trip to the Kruger National Park is unique. Enjo the experience, respect the rules, and you are sure to have a unforgettable adventure!

12 Practical trips when travelling to Johannesbur and the surrounding provinces

When traveling to Cape Town, here are some practical informatio and travel tips to keep in mind. Some of these have been discusse but a reminder is well worth while.

12.1 Understanding the Weather and Climate

Johannesburg has a mild climate, but it can get quite cold in winte (June to August), so pack accordingly. The summer month (November to February) are warm and can be quite rainy, so it is good idea to pack a raincoat or umbrella.

12.2 Safety Precautions

While Johannesburg is a vibrant city with much to offer, it i important to be aware of your surroundings and take common-sens precautions. Avoid displaying expensive jewelry or electronics an be cautious when walking around at night. Use reputable tax services or ride-sharing apps for transportation.

12.3 Health Considerations

Johannesburg is not a malaria area, but if you're planning to visit game reserves in other parts of the country, you may need to take malaria prophylaxis. Consult with your doctor before your trip. Also, remember to stay hydrated, especially during the hot summer months.

12.4 Cultural Sensitivity

South Africa is a diverse country with many different cultures. Respect local customs and traditions and be open to learning about the country's rich cultural heritage.

12.5 Exploring the Surrounding Provinces

If you're planning to visit other provinces, keep in mind that distances can be quite large in South Africa. Plan your itinerary accordingly and make sure you have a reliable means of transportation. Many tourists rent a car for the duration of their stay but remember that South Africans drive on the left side of the road.

12.6 Visiting Game Reserves

When visiting game reserves, remember to respect the wildlife. Keep a safe distance, do not feed the animals, and stay in your vehicle unless in a designated area. Also, pack binoculars for better game viewing.

12.7 Tipping

Tipping is customary in South Africa. In restaurants, a tip of 10-15% is standard. It's also customary to tip tour guides, drivers, and hotel staff.

12.8 Shopping

South Africa has a value-added tax (VAT) of 15%, which is included in the price of goods. As a tourist, you can claim back this tax at the airport upon departure, so keep your receipts if you plan to do this.

12.9 Enjoy Your Visit

Above all, enjoy your visit to Johannesburg and the surrounding provinces. South Africa is a beautiful country with a rich history, diverse cultures, and stunning landscapes. Whether you're exploring the bustling city of Johannesburg, visiting historical sites, or spotting wildlife in a game reserve, there's something for everyone in this vibrant country.

13 Conclusion

Johannesburg, the vibrant heart of South Africa, and Mpumalanga, the province of the rising sun, together offer an unforgettable travel experience. From the bustling streets of Johannesburg with its rich history and cultural diversity, to the breathtaking natural beauty and wildlife of Mpumalanga, there is a wealth of experiences waiting to be discovered.

Johannesburg, with its mix of modern urban life and historical significance, offers a unique insight into South Africa's past while also showcasing its dynamic future. The city's museums, art galleries, markets, and restaurants provide a rich tapestry of experiences that reflect the city's diverse cultures and history.

A short drive away, Mpumalanga offers a stark contrast with its stunning landscapes, majestic wildlife, and tranquil atmosphere. The province is home to some of South Africa's most spectacular natural attractions, including the Blyde River Canyon, God's Window, and numerous waterfalls. It's also the gateway to the world-renowned Kruger National Park, where you can experience the thrill of spotting the Big Five in their natural habitat.

Whether you are a history buff, a nature lover, a foodie, or an adventure seeker, Johannesburg and Mpumalanga offer a multitude of experiences that cater to all interests and tastes. The warmth and hospitality of the people you will meet along the way will make your journey even more memorable.

In conclusion, a trip to Johannesburg and Mpumalanga offers a unique blend of urban exploration and natural beauty, providing a comprehensive and diverse experience of what South Africa has to offer. It's a journey of discovery that leaves a lasting impression, beckoning travelers to return and explore more of this beautiful and diverse country.

Thank you, Dankie, Kea Leboha!

Printed in Great Britain
by Amazon

59076268R00069